LIVERPOOL MURDERS – KIRKD.
1870-1891

Introduction

Between 1831 and 1867 a total of 31 people were hanged publicly at Kirkdale gaol, in front of crowds ranging from 500 to 100,000. The Capital Punishment Amendment Act of 1868 put an end to public executions in the United Kingdom, but the hangings that carried on in private were so near the walls that it was said by those outside that a thud could be heard when the trapdoor opened.

Between 1870 and the gaol's closure in 1892, there were 29 condemned prisoners hanged at Kirkdale. The number of crimes totalled 26, with three of the hangings being for killings that involved more than one murderer, The most notorious of them was in 1884 when two sisters from the slums of Vauxhall in Liverpool were hanged for killings that were motivated by the desire to claim insurance money.

Many of those condemned were from slum properties and lived lives of squalor where drink seemed their only escape, fuelling angry misjudgements which would ultimately lead to them standing on the scaffold. Just under half of the killings detailed here (12) involved a man or woman killing their spouse or partner. The majority were following drinking bouts but there were exceptions, such as the case in Widnes where Patrick Kearns and Hugh Burns killed the husband of Kearns's lover. In three of the murders the victim was another family member such as a parent or aunt, while others were more random with work colleagues or passers by being the victims,

Some of the killings described here have a stark resemblance to today, with two of them involving men killing children who were loosely known to them. The case of William Fish was a particularly brutal one, with the victim being a seven year old girl who was raped and beheaded. What was even more shocking about this was the fact Fish had children of his own and police interviewed him but didn't look hard for the clues that might have seen him arrested immediately. Those hanged were aged between seventeen and sixty although there could have been an even younger convict, as in 1886 a sixteen year old who killed a work colleague who had bullied him saw his death sentence commuted.

Whereas many of those publicly hanged at Kirkdale had committed murders in the Manchester area, the vast majority of those hanged in private were for killings in and around Liverpool. In 1864 Manchester had become an assize town meaning that now Liverpool was dealing mainly with cases from its own area and western Lancashire. There were some occasions though when for capacity issues, a Manchester case was heard in Liverpool. After the closure of Kirkdale gaol in 1892 Walton gaol became the place were those convicted at Liverpool were hanged, with over 60 taking place prior to the last execution there in 1964.

In compiling this book I have put the details of these murders together using newspaper reports of the time as my only source. Any similarity to other articles on the internet is purely coincidental.

The circumstances behind the first private execution at Kirkdale were very similar to so those that had led to many of the public ones. John Gregson, who habitually got drunk and abused his wife, was hanged after kicking her to death after being discharged from court earlier in the day.

28 year old collier Gregson had married his wife Ellen, two years his junior, in 1863. She was subjected to frequent beatings from him and on one occasion he was even imprisoned for six months. However she found it in her to forgive him but even when she borne him two children he didn't change his ways. In total he appeared before the courts 24 times in the 1860s for drunken and disorderly behaviour.

The last of those frequent appearances was on 18th October 1869 when Gregson was fined for drunkenness. The penalty was paid by Ellen and they went to a few pubs before returning to their home at Wood's Yard, where a lodger was looking after the two children. Ellen started to breastfeed their sixteen month old infant and two neighbours called in as Gregson sat sulkily on the stairs.

After a few minutes Gregson took his jacket off and asked one of the neighbours, Mrs Littler, to take it to the pawn shop for him and she said she would do so the following day. Gregson took it back saying he would do it himself and then Ellen stood up and told him to wait a few minutes and she would take it. Gregson then took the baby and demanded she bring him a pint of beer straightaway or he would kick her. Ellen said she would pawn the jacket for food but not drink, leading to him running at her and lashing out with his foot, causing her to fall.

Whilst Ellen was on the floor Gregson continued to rain kicks on her in the back, side and chest. The other neighbour who was there Mr Hilton managed to intervene and push him down onto a chair, then try to lift Ellen up. However Gregson was soon off the chair and kicked out again, catching the back of her head with his clogged foot. As blood foamed out of her ears and mouth the callous husband got a shovel and spread ashes over it and when told by Hilton that he had killed her replied 'If I haven't I ought to.'

Ellen was still alive and was put to bed, where Gregson joined her and soon fell asleep despite her moans. The following day he went for some brandy but she was unable to drink it as the teeth had clenched together. He did though pawn his jacket for ten shillings so a doctor could be paid, but Ellen died two days later on 21st October, having continually complained of her head being in agony. A post mortem revealed a fracture at the base of the skull, with Ellen's body otherwise being healthy. The inquest returned a verdict of wilful murder leading to Gregson being committed for trial.

Gregson was tried at the assizes on 20th December and wept while much of the evidence was presented. His defence was an inventive one, his counsel Mr Torr telling the jury that as he regularly beat his wife as a matter of routine it showed there was no intent to kill so he was only guilty of manslaughter. The judge Baron Martin though directed the jury differently, saying if they accepted the evidence of Mr Hilton and Mrs Littler then he was guilty of murder or nothing at all. After some deliberation and clarification of the law from the judge the jury found Gregson guilty of murder, but with a recommendation for mercy as two members were of the opinion that he had not intended to cause death by his actions.

In sentencing Gregson to death Baron Martin said that he had no more doubt that this was a case of murder than he had of his own existence and that 'it was about as clear a case of murder than was ever proved.' Despite the jury's recommendation Gregson never believed he had any hope of a reprieve and on

31st December he wrote to his family asking for a final meeting and saying that he had repented and would die a Christian, hoping that it would be enough to take him to Heaven.

Mr Pigott, the chaplain of the gaol regularly attended to Gregson, who repented, deplored his love of drink and accepted the justness of his sentence. He did maintain there had been no intent to kill and urged the chaplain to explain the consequences of drink to many of his fellow colliers who were in the gaol, for offences committed whilst drunk. In his last week before the sentence was to be carried out he was visited by his mother and also Ellen's father, who brought his two children who would soon become orphaned due to his dreadful deed.

On Saturday 8th January 1870 the gaol's governor Mr Gibbs conveyed the news that the Home Secretary could see no grounds for a reprieve and Gregson accepted this with good grace. Whereas the public executions used to take place on Saturdays at noon, legislation now stated that they would take place at 8am on the third Monday after the assize judges had left the town. The scaffold that was used was the same as had been used previously and was erected on the Saturday afternoon. William Calcraft the executioner arrived at 7pm on the Sunday and slept inside the gaol grounds in a special dormitory.

Gregson rose at 630am on the day of the execution and was taken to the chaplain's private room where he engaged in devotional exercises. At 745am the prison bell tolled a funeral knell and Calcraft went to collect the prisoner, who submitted himself firmly to pinioning. The procession then began led by the governor and followed by the chaplain, Gregson, Calcraft, a visiting justice, the Under-Sheriff of Lancashire and some other officials. The *Daily Post* reported how the private nature of the execution, free of unruly crowds gave it a much more solemn air, with people speaking in no more than a whisper. Outside there were none of the 'denizens of the lowest purlieus of Liverpool', instead just half a dozen policemen and a few interested onlookers waiting for the black flag to be hoisted.

As 8am approached Gregson suddenly started to shake his hands uncontrollably and twitch his lips, his face going a deathly shade of pale. As the rope was placed around his neck he said 'Lord Jesus receive my soul' before Calcraft shook his hand, placed a hood over his head then stepped back and pulled the bolt. Gregson dropped and was dead after three or four slight writhings. At 10am an inquest was held and the body then buried in the precints of the gaol.

8th January 1873 – Richard Spencer, For the Murder of Elizabeth Wharton at Liverpool

The first Liverpool murderer to be hanged privately in Kirkdale was a man who killed a lover that was only half his age. He then had to endure the agony of his execution being postponed just two days before schedule due to the hangman being required elsewhere.

Richard Spencer was born in 1812 and was brought up by his grandparents after his mother and father emigrated to Australia when he was five years old. They wished for him to join them and sent funds over to England, but he chose not to go there. At the age of sixteen he married in Manchester and remained with his wife for nearly 25 years before separating, both accusing the other of too much drunkenness.

Whilst in his mid forties Spencer got involved with Elizabeth Wharton, who lived in Liscard but travelled to Liverpool every day to hawk fish and poultry. Spencer was quite well off as he ran his own fishmonger business and he persuaded Elizabeth, who he described as 'a fine buxom Cheshire lass' to live with him despite her still being in her teens. For fifteen years they lived happily together in Breck Road where Spencer's business was a success, but towards the end of the 1860s things weren't so successful. This, coupled with Elizabeth turning to drink led to Spencer becoming depressed and in ill health, leading to him going to see his sister in Yorkshire in the summer of 1872.

To raise funds when Spencer was away Elizabeth sold much of the furniture and also some valuable pictures, which was particularly upsetting for him. When he returned they lived in Coniston Street for a brief period and then moved to Gregson Street, where he intended to start up in business again. Spencer was jealous of Elizabeth's friendships with other men although there was no hint of what horror would take place early in the morning of 9th August when he shot her before attempting suicide.

The couple went to bed on the previous evening without having had a drink, but about 7am Elizabeth was awoken by a blow to the head, with Spencer saying he wanted them to die together. She managed to get away to a neighbour, who dressed her wound and then they went to the property and found him with a wound to the forehead and bleeding from the ear. Spencer begged Elizabeth to kiss him and she did so then the police were called and on their arrival, he handed the officer a revolver and begged him to put him out of his misery.

Both were taken to the Royal Infirmary, where Elizabeth was able to give a deposition stating that Spencer was a heavy drinker who had often threatened to kill her, leading to her sleeping with a knife under her pillow. She denied ever being unfaithful and died three days later. Spencer recovered and was handed over to the police on 26th September, saying as he was committed for trial that Elizabeth's drunken habits had led to his furniture being sold.

At his trial Spencer wore a bandage around his head. He claimed that he was trying to shoot himself but missed, causing a bullet to hit Elizabeth instead. However this didn't convince the jury and he was found guilty and sentenced to death with Justice Mellor telling him to hold little hope of mercy.

Spencer fully acknowledged the situation he was in and showed penitence to the gaol chaplain Reverend Pigott. He did though maintain he had not intended to kill Elizabeth and must have been out of his mind, as he loved her too much even though she was the ruin of him. He received numerous visits from friends and also his ex wife. His execution was fixed for Monday 6th January 1873 but on that morning it was discovered that William Calcraft, who had been at the gaol on the Saturday checking everything was in order, was now hanging a convict at Durham.

When Spencer was told of the postponement he was distraught, especially as he thought a reprieve was being communicated to him.

On 8th January Spencer was woken by the gaol governor having spent a restless night. He took some light refreshment then prayed fervently. At 745am the bell tolled and he was taken through the drizzle to the scaffold saying 'Lord have mercy on my soul.' On seeing the equipment that would take him to his death Spencer reeled in terror and he had to be helped under the beam by two turnkeys. As Calcraft placed the hood over his head and adjusted the noose the condemned man said 'Lord Jesus receive my soul' and the bolt was drawn. Calcraft had calculated everything perfectly and he died with scarcely a struggle.

The hanging of Richard Spencer may have gone smoothly but the same can't be said for that of James Connor, who had killed a Good Samaritan that tried to intervene as he assaulted a woman. William Calcraft made a serious miscalculation leading to the rope snapping and the condemned man having to be brought up and hanged again.

On Monday 11th August 1873 Mary Shears, the wife of a ship's steward, attended the Cambridge Music Hall in Mill Street, Toxteth, where she was spotted by 29 year old James Connor who asked her to join him for a drink. She declined but at the end of the performance he followed her and at the corner of Jackson and Mill Streets he accused her of taking some money from him. Shears said that Connor was mistaken and he then struck her twice, causing her to fall to the floor.

The incident was witnessed by a 40 year old man named James Gaffney and he and his friend William Metcalf crossed the road to assist. Gaffney asked why Connor had done what he did, leading to Connor taking a knife from his pocket and stabbing him in the neck. He then took off his jacket saying he was ready for a fight but Metcalf punched him to the ground. Connor got back up and thrust the knife at him, but it didn't cut through the clothing. Connor then walked briskly away but Metcalf found a police officer and the two of them chased after and apprehended him.

Gaffney was helped by Susannah Burke, who had also been asked for a drink by Connor in the theatre. He was taken to the Southern Hospital where he was found to have lost a large quantity of blood and was also insensible. An operation was performed immediately but he died the following morning and a post mortem revealed that the knife had penetrated the spine. The inquest took place on 13th August and a number of people who had been in the area told how they had not seen any provocation from Gaffney or Metcalf. This led to a verdict of wilful murder being returned and Connor was committed for trial at the assizes, which were taking place the following week.

On 18th August it was proved that Connor's knife, which he had kept in his pocket after the incident, had caused the wound from which Gaffney died while witnesses again confirmed that Gaffney and Metcalf had acted in a reasonable manner. His defence counsel argued that a manslaughter verdict would be more appropriate as there had been no pre mediation and also there was a hint of provocation. In summing up though the judge said provocation could only be deemed to have happened if the jury were satisfied that Gaffney had touched Connor. After half an hours deliberation the jury told the judge that they could not reach a verdict but he refused to discharge them and Connor even told them to look sharp and stop keeping him waiting. It took a further hour for them to find him guilty of murder.

Connor had shown total indifference during his trial and remained unmoved as Justice Brett sentenced him to death, saying that he had acted with 'cruel and cowardly brutality.' Calling it an 'unpardonable murder' Justice Brett told him he could see no reason why there should be mitigating circumstances and that he should make use of the short time he had left to ask for mercy from God. The *Liverpool Mercury* described Connor's family members who had attended the trial as 'most respectable people'. He had been born in Ireland and raised in London, then worked in Birmingham and Sheffield before arriving in Liverpool. As a boilermaker he could earn up to £1 a day, but he got into the wrong crowd and spent most of his time drinking, making money from boxing and wrestling instead.

After his arrival in the condemned cell Connor continued to show callous indifference to his fate and initially refused to be attended to by Father Bonte. His attitude though did soften and he began to engage in prayers and requested a visit from his mother who was living in Sheffield. She came to see him but a second visit planned for the Saturday before the execution was too much for her to bear and only his sister attended. She brought along with her a letter from their mother urging him to make peace with the Maker.

The execution was fixed for 8th September but the day before there was some confusion as to who would be carrying it out. It was believed that Calcraft had retired but the gaol had not been given any official notification of any replacement. Late on the Sunday night 73 year old Calcraft did arrive and on receiving confirmation that it was going ahead Connor went to bed early and slept soundly, rising at 530am. After receiving the sacrament from Father Bonte he had a hearty breakfast then returned to prayer.

At 730am the governor Captain Gibbs admitted the press and checked their credentials, as it had became apparent at the previous execution there that two members of the public had gained admittance when they had no right to be there. The bell tolled at 745am and shortly before the hour Connor was pinioned, assisting those who did so with the process. He walked firmly to the scaffold and smiled at warders as he climbed the steps, being by far the coolest of those present. Calcraft placed the hood over his head and adjusted the rope but after pulling the bolt the rope snapped and Connor fell straight to the floor. He was helped up by two warders and sat in a chair suffering pain in his neck where the rope marks had drawn blood, while Calcraft paced about in an agitated fashion examining the rope.

Connor paid little attention as Father Bonte read religious texts to him, instead telling the warders: 'Do you call this murder, you should let me off after this this is surely enough.' Around eight minutes later though Calcraft was ready to try again and Connor offered no resistance, pulling the hood over his head himself and assisting the executioner as he put the rope around his neck. The second attempt saw Connor struggle intensely after the bolt was drawn and he died a painful death. After an hour the body was cut down and an inquest held, where no blame was apportioned to the gaol officials or Calcraft for the failed first attempt. Gaol officials though did suggest he may have miscalculated the prisoner's weight. Calcraft had been particularly unnerved by the incident and said nothing except when giving his evidence to the jury. He left Liverpool for London on the 1050am train.

The routineness of domestic violence in Victorian Liverpool was no more exemplified than by the murder of Mary Corrigan by her son Thomas. He paid the ultimate price at Kirkdale for battering her to death after she was late making his supper, a murder that horrified even the most hardened in the crime ridden neighbourhood where it took place.

23 year old Thomas Corrigan, a dock porter, lived in Chisenhale Street with his parents Patrick and Mary, and three adult lodgers. They were a single man named James Canavan and a married couple called Richard and Johanna Harris, who had two young children. Three months before the murder and against his mother's approval Corrigan moved Martha Knight, who he had been seeing eight years, into the house.

On the afternoon of Saturday 1st November 1873, Corrigan went drinking then returned to his home with Knight and went upstairs. This led to Mary, who was making tea for her lodgers, to complain to them about what she saw as his immoral behaviour. Corrigan heard this and at about 630pm he got up and demanded his supper from Mary, who told him it was in the oven. When Corrigan opened the oven door and saw nothing was there he punched her to the floor before kicking her, pulling her hair and smashing her face against the floor. When his father tried to stop the attack Corrigan struck him and he left the house, leaving the rest of the occupants at the mercy of the son over whom he had no control.

Corrigan grabbed hold of Richard Harris but apologised although James Canavan was not so lucky, being punched to the ground even though he described himself as a cripple. He managed to escape as well and Corrigan then bolted and locked the door before climbing on the table from where he jumped onto his mother and then danced on her as she lay in a state of unconsciousness. He then called for Knight to bring him some water which he threw over Mary to revive her, leading to her telling him that he was a good boy. He then demanded money and ripped her clothes off to see if there was any there. For no particular reason he then began attacking Knight with his belt and Mary seized the opportunity to crawl upstairs but Corrigan followed her to Mr and Mrs Harris's room, where she had sought refuge. He set about his mother with his belt, hitting her face with the buckle and then pushed her down the stairs. He then went down and stamped on her again until she was senseless, before grabbing a kitchen knife and holding it to her throat, saying he may as well be hung for her.

Despite Mary's screams no neighbours contacted police, probably because such sounds were commonplace in the vicinity, especially of a Saturday evening. Chisenhale Street was a notorious hotbed of crime and vice, being one of the streets that connected the docks with Scotland Road via its bridge over the canal.

When Corrigan had finally finished the assault Mary was placed in bed and a priest sent for, who was told by him that she had fallen down the stairs. The priest, Father Ross, didn't believe Corrigan's story and on leaving the property went to the Chisenhale Street Bridewell, telling the desk sergeant of his suspicions. Police Constable McDowell was dispatched to the property and met Corrigan in the street, who said that Mary had died suddenly. McDowell immediately arrested Corrigan and sent for Inspector McAuley from the Dale Street Bridewell, who found a frightful sight on arrival at 30 Chisenhale Street. Mary's face was mashed to a pulp, her eyeball was ruptured, hair was all over the floor and ribs were broken.

Corrigan was charged with murder and replied 'No sir you are wrong, who can prove that? I only came to the officer to get a doctor.' The doctor who arrived and carried out a post mortem established that the cause of death was a fractured skull. He also saw Corrigan at the Bridewell and found him to be quite sober. The following day, thousands of people came to Chisenhale Street to look at the house where the atrocity had occurred, with Mary's body remaining inside under police guard until an inquest could take place. The following day an inquest returned a verdict of wilful murder the coroner commenting that it was 'one of the most diabolical and revolting murders that had ever disgraced the annals of this country.'

After being committed to the assizes Corrigan was tried before Justice Quain on 16th December. Mr and Mrs Harris told how the attack unfolded and how there had been no provocation whatsoever from Mary. They also said how they had seen him violent before, even though they had only lodged there three weeks. On one night they thought Corrigan was going to kill Knight and he seemed to spend most of his time drinking, having worked only two days in the time they had been there. In cross examination Mr Harris was accused of being a coward by Corrigan's counsel for staying in his room during the second phase of the attack and not intervening even though he was bigger. Canavan described Corrigan as somebody who always wanted to fight after a drink and as having a 'wild excited look' as he came down the stairs.

Martha Knight was also a witness and she told how she had heard Mary criticising their relationship and that she closed the door in the hope Corrigan wouldn't hear her. When he woke, he suddenly developed a great fury and quickly got up and ran downstairs. She often had to be asked to speak up when giving her evidence and seemed to be in a state of mourning, having borne Corrigan two children. Dr Donovan gave evidence in relation to the injuries and also said that if Corrigan was suffering from delirium tremens, then he would not have been so clam when he saw him in the police station.

Corrigan's defence counsel claimed that the crime had taken place during a 'fit of horrors' due to alcohol and as such he should only be found guilty of manslaughter. However in summing up Justice Quain said that there was no evidence to suggest insanity and his statement about being hung for her implied that he knew what he was doing. After ten minutes deliberation the jury returned a verdict of guilty of murder. Corrigan replied that he had nothing to say when asked and was told by the judge that his mother was somebody he was 'bound to love and cherish' prior to being sentenced to death. He said the crime had 'disclosed such a state of brutality so shocking that I have never heard anything like it before.' Quain told him to expect no mercy and the following day the *Liverpool Mercury* wrote that the case was 'unique in the annals of atrocity' and that 'never before has a more fearful story of human depravity, brute strength and determined cruelty been told'.

Whilst awaiting execution at Kirkdale Corrigan was attended to by Father Bonte and held out hope of a reprieve, but it was never a realistic prospect and nobody appealed on his behalf. He was visited by his sister and father, who forgave him for the crime and requested the prison take a photograph of his son so he could have a keepsake.

After receiving the communion on Sunday 4th January 1874 Corrigan slept soundly, getting up at 645am. In a move from normal procedure, the gaol officials had decided that as soon as they were up condemned men would go to the gaol reception room, which was just a few feet from the scaffold and removed the need for a procession of around 100 metres. Corrigan had his breakfast there and at 7am Father Bonte arrived, the two then engaging in fervent prayer and not breaking from that when the prison bell tolled at 745am.

With William Calcraft being engaged in a triple hanging at Durham, the executioner on this occasion was Mr Anderson, who refused to divulge his first name. Pinioning took place in the reception room and Corrigan was then taken onto the scaffold, where Mr Anderson did not undertake Calcraft's tradition of shaking the prisoner's hand. After the bolt was drawn Corrigan was said by one journalist to have muttered 'oh' immediately on dropping through the trapdoor, but his death was swift and any further movement over the next three to four minutes was put down to muscle contractions. As was customary, the body was left hanging for an hour and then buried in the precints of then prison.

31st August 1874 – Henry Flanagan, For the Murder of Mary Flanagan at Liverpool & Mary Williams, For the Murder of Nicholas Manning at Bootle

The first double hanging that took place in private at Kirkdale involved killers that had both killed family members. The case of Henry Flanagan was a particularly wicked one and he attracted little sympathy, but there was a good deal of outcry over that of Mary Williams, who was a mother of seven children and the first woman to be hanged there for thirty years.

21 year old Henry Flanagan was originally from Leitrim in Ireland and was taken to Glasgow by his parents at the age of 15. He married a Scottish woman with whom he had a daughter in 1872. As a shoemaker he would often travel for work, which brought him to Liverpool where he was employed by his aunt Mary Flanagan at Bent Street. This was situated where there is now grass landscaping opposite the junction of Scotland Road and Leeds Street. Mary was a stout 53 year old widow who employed four shoemakers, with Flanagan acting as the foreman.

On Saturday 4th April the four employees finished work about 4pm and sent for ale, drinking at the shop premises along with Mary until around 11pm when they were well and truly intoxicated. Flanagan was then seen by Mary to drop a pair of her shoes, leading to her claiming he intended pawning them to get more drink as he had been saying he had no money. This enraged him but things soon calmed down and other members of the household either went out or to bed, leaving Flanagan and Mary alone in the kitchen.

Flanagan then raped and strangled Mary before going to sleep on a trickle bed, leaving her lying on the floor. At around 5am a female lodger came down to light the fire but didn't notice that Mary was dead and she returned to her room none the wiser. Soon after this Flanagan went to bed and Mary's cold body was found a few hours later, next to a purse from which £3 to £4 had been taken. When Flanagan was woken at around 8am to be told his aunt was dead, he gave the news an extremely calm reaction. He simply got his coat and stated to others that he was going to Manchester and invited one of them, George O'Neill, to go with him.

An examination of Mary's body found she had died of suffocation and also appeared to have been strangled. There was also evidence that she had been violated sexually and Flanagan's description was quickly circulated around police stations across the area.

At Lime Street station Flanagan was told that there was no train for another six hours and he said he had to be out of town earlier and would walk instead. At a shop Flanagan bought some tobacco and paid with a gold sovereign, telling the keeper not to hand him back the change (19 shillings) as he had plenty of money. Both men walked as far as Prescot, stopping for ale several times along the way which Flanagan paid for. He was suddenly flush with money despite having none the night before and admitted to having 'had a tussle with the old woman.' When the men reached Prescot, Flanagan announced that he was going to try and get to Glasgow but instead walked back towards Liverpool.

At about 9pm that night Flanagan was found in a drunken state on a footpath by a policeman in Knotty Ash. He said that he had been walking from Manchester since the Friday and was near death from starvation. He was taken to Old Swan police station where it was found that his description matched that of the man wanted for Mary's murder and he was charged, telling the officer 'it cannot be helped now.' The following Friday an inquest returned a verdict of wilful murder against Flanagan, who was committed for trial at the next assizes.

At his trial on 14th and 15th August Flanagan's defence counsel argued that the evidence against him was purely circumstantial, the evidence of O'Neill was unreliable and death could instead have come from apoplexy. However the fact Mary's purse was empty, his waistcoat was next to her body and he was in possession of a substantial amount of money helped the jury convict him after just a few minutes deliberation. Justice Archibald then sentenced him to death, lamenting that again drunkenness was a factor and suggesting it accounted for a third to half of all crimes. A few days after his trial Flanagan was visited at Kirkdale by his wife, child and parents, who had all travelled from Glasgow. He made a confession to them that he had ravished, robbed and strangled his aunt, but there was no intent to kill.

Flanagan was tended to by Father Bonte while awaiting his fate, as was fellow Roman Catholic Mary Williams. The mother of seven had been condemned to death after shooting a man dead at Bootle following an argument with some neighbours.

Williams was Irish born and lived in Raleigh Street with her husband, to whom she had been married ten years, most of them unhappily. She was regularly in trouble and in 1872 was sentenced to seven days imprisonment for non payment of a fine.

On 20th April 1874 Williams got into an argument with some female neighbours who set about beating her. The brother of one of the women was Nicholas Manning, who later that evening was seen in the street by Williams who threw cups at hi. This caused him to run away towards his father's house, shouting that he had never struck a woman in his life. Later on he was back and Williams produced a revolver from under her apron and fired it at him, before handing herself over to police and saying that she had done it and would do it again. Manning was taken to Bootle Borough Hospital where he died two weeks later.

Williams maintained at her trial on 13th August that she had only intended to frighten Manning and not cause him harm, but she was found guilty of murder. Her husband, a 27 year old dock labourer, told authorities he was unable to cope and handed six of their seven children over to the workhouse at Walton before going missing. The youngest, aged just eight months, was allowed to stay with Williams in gaol until she had been weaned before joining her siblings in the workhouse.

Despite numerous pleas, including by the Mayor of Bootle, for the sentence to be commuted to life imprisonment the Home Secretary refused to grant a reprieve to Williams meaning she would be the first woman to be hanged at Kirkdale since poisoner Betty Eccles in 1843. There were heartbreaking scenes when Williams said goodbye to her children when they were brought from the workhouse to see her three days before she was due to die.

Both the condemned culprits went to bed at 9pm the night before the execution, which was to take place on Monday 31st August. Neither slept much though and both refused breakfast after getting up. By 630am they were in the chapel receiving the communion from Father Bonte. As the press were being admitted at 730am a man came running across the fields demanding to see Flanagan. The request was refused and he left, telling journalists that he was a 'very good mate.'

As Williams walked towards the scaffold she turned to the assembled journalists and said 'Gentleman on my conscience it was my husband who fired that pistol.' As she was about to speak further she was given a gentle nudge by an official and continued her slow walk, praying fervently. Flanagan, described by the *Liverpool Mercury* as having led a 'dissolute, wicked life' which led to a 'deplorable level of depravity.' then appeared from another door. He looked across to the press as if he was about to say something but instead just stood still on the scaffold.

The hangman was William Marwood from Lincolnshire, who strapped Flanagan's legs together tightly then received assistance from the condemned man in putting the rope around his neck. Before the cap was put over his head Flanagan looked up as if to heaven, then he had to wait while Marwood got Williams ready. She asked to speak but the request was denied and as she was being pinioned she recited the Lord's Prayer and then said 'God pardon me for all my bygones.' Just as she was about to say a 'Hail Mary' the bolt was drawn and both dropped to their deaths, which were instantaneous. The black flag was then hoisted outside the prison to indicate that the sentence had been carried out.

<u>4th January 1875 – John McCrave & Michael Mullen, For the Murder of Richard Morgan at Liverpool, & William Worthington, For the Murder of Ann Worthington at Liverpool.</u>

The next execution at Kirkdale was a triple one which included two young men being hanged for a brutal killing in Tithebarn Street that attracted national notoriety. They met their fate alongside a man who had killed his wife in yet another case where drink fuelled assault ended in death.

Richard Morgan's death at the hands of a group of youths who kicked him like a football was particularly shocking due to the complete overreaction of those responsible just because they were refused money, as well as the number of bystanders who did not intervene. It happened on an August Bank Holiday evening after the 26 year old shop assistant had been on a day out to New Ferry and led to the press writing some savage words on those who loitered around Liverpool's street corners.

Recently married Morgan had been to a Druids gala with his new wife Alice and brother Samuel on Monday 3rd August 1874. On returning to Liverpool at about 9pm they had a quick drink in Chapel Street then walked up Tithebarn Street on their way to their Leeds Street home. When 20 year old John McCrave asked them for 6d for ale as they passed a pub at the corner of Lower Milk Street Morgan suggested that he work for his money like others. The response of McCrave was to punch Morgan to the ground then his fellow roughs Peter Campbell and Michael Mullen (aged 19 and 17 respectively) joined in kicking him about the head. Morgan's brother bravely tried to intervene and knocked Mullen down, but he had a knife pulled on him by McCrave and his brother's situation was already helpless.

A crowd of up to 100 gathered after hearing the screams of Morgan's wife, who had only been married to him for two months. However rather than intervene they just watched, some of them cheering as Morgan was kicked forty feet down the street. A police constable arrived and they dispersed, but after brandy failed to revive him Morgan was taken to the Northern Dispensary in Vauxhall Road where he was pronounced dead on arrival. McCrave was followed by Samuel to his residence in nearby Hatton Garden, leading to his apprehension the same evening. He was well known to the police as one of the many 'cornermen' in the town, who would loiter outside pubs demanding money with menaces from passers by. Also known as John Quinn, he had only recently come out of gaol after serving nine months for burglary.

A post mortem revealed that Morgan had a heart defect but this would not have caused death. Three surgeons determined that he had died of shock caused by the brutality of the kicking, which had gone on for ten minutes and left his torso black and blue. This led to an inquest verdict of wilful murder and he was interred at Smithdown Road cemetery the following Saturday, at which time the two other suspects remained at large. The murder made headlines nationwide and became known as the 'Tithebarn Street Outrage'. An opinion in *The Times* stated: 'The worst and most hopeless part of the story was that Richard Morgan was knocked down and kicked to death in the presence of a considerable crowd. No one seems to have thought it was their business to interfere. The crowd was enjoying the struggle, hounding on the murderers and encouraging them to greater violence.'

Samuel Morgan told police he could identify those who had assisted McCrave and some members of the community did give names in. Michael Mullen was captured on 14th August, having attempted to stowaway on board a vessel bound for Philadelphia with his 15 year old brother. When found he was transferred to another ship and returned to Liverpool, where he replied 'No not me' when charged by police. Alice Morgan was there to meet the vessel and positively identified Mullen as one of those involved, while his brother Thomas was charged with being an accessory after the fact.

At the end of the August the government offered a £100 reward for any information that would lead to the capture of Peter Campbell. On 11th September a tip off was received that he had been working in a mine near Bolton but when police went to arrest him at this lodgings, they handcuffed his landlord instead allowing Campbell to escape. Unbelievably he made his way to Liverpool where he visited McCrave's sister Mary, to whom he had a child. He openly drank in the area but in the early hours of 13th December a man went into the detective office in Dale Street to say he was in a court in Gascoyne Street. Five officers went there and found Campbell hiding under a bed. He went quietly and told officers he was there but didn't carry out any kicking and had also intended to sail to Melbourne. An identity parade involving nine others took place and after being picked out by Alice he was formally charged.

The three males appeared before the stipendiary magistrate on 14th September and were committed to the next assizes. Thomas Mullen was discharged, the magistrate telling him that what he did was wrong but his time on remand had been punishment enough. They stood trial before Mr Justice Mellor on 14th December with Samuel and Alice giving evidence, the latter weeping as she did so. The defence counsel suggested that their version of events had been grossly exaggerated and as there had been no motive or premeditation, a manslaughter verdict was more appropriate. However all three, who showed a complete indifference to what was going on, were found guilty of murder and sentenced to death although there was a recommendation of mercy for Campbell whose role hadn't been as great as the others.

As he left the courtroom McCrave shouted to the public gallery that people should 'keep from drink.' Outside the court as the prison van drove them to Kirkdale a female who was believed to be related to them shouted that it was wrong that three should be hanged for the death of one. Families of the guilty men petitioned the Home Secretary for reprieves but few people amongst the general public supported them and a side petition calling for the gang members to be flogged to death received lukewarm support. It was not until two days before the execution that Campbell had his sentence commuted to life imprisonment, to the relief of his widowed mother who was a respectable shopkeeper.

The murder of Ann Worthington by her husband was not so sensational and sadly one of a kind that was all too common at the time. Originally from Scarisbrick, William Worthington was a 33 year old 'flatman', employed on a flat bottomed horse drawn canal boat that carried coal between Liverpool and Wigan. He lived on board along with Ann, their two young children and her daughter from a previous marriage that had left her widowed.

On 29th August 1874 a woman in Vauxhall Road heard screams going on for a quarter of an hour and when she looked out of her window she saw Ann crouched down in a yard where flatmen tethered their horses. Worthington was standing over her, kicking away at her body. The woman and a male passer by both tried to get him to stop but were told to mind their own business, leading to the male whistling for a policeman.

Even though Ann's face was covered with mud and blood and she was in a distressed state, the policeman who arrived on the scene took no action when told they were man and wife. Instead he told the couple to go home and make it up, even when Ann asked the officer to take her husband away. The brutality had taken place due to him being unhappy that she gave him only a shilling when he asked for some money.

On getting back on board the boat, which was moored under the bridge at Boundary Street, Worthington continued his assault in front of Ann's daughter, administering one kick into her abdomen that was so hard it broke the stay-bone of her corset. He then went asleep but continued his assault the next morning, hitting Ann with a poker. Ann managed to get away and stayed for a week with a well-wisher called Mrs Duffy in Hopwood Street before being taken to her sister's address in Wigan. Whilst there her condition deteriorated and she died at 4am on 10th September, having suffered a broken collarbone, ribs and severe internal injuries.

The terrible deed was unprovoked and no doubt driven by drink, which turned Worthington from being a kind man devoted to his family to someone in a complete rage. He was arrested in Wigan the same day that Ann died and taken to Liverpool a few days later, telling the police officer who transferred him that it was a 'bad job' and that he wouldn't have done it for a thousand pounds now.

Worthington was tried on 16th December, the medical evidence showing that Ann had died from pleuropneumonia aggravated by violence. The only defence that could be offered was that he did not intend to cause death but he was found guilty of murder with a recommendation for mercy. Justice Mellor passed sentence in the usual form and said that he would forward the recommendation to he Home Secretary.

Whilst in Kirkdale awaiting his fate Worthington seemed confident of a reprieve, acknowledging his crime but not believing it merited the most extreme sentence of the law. However, although Patrick Campbell was notified on 2nd January that his sentence had been commuted, nothing was forthcoming for Wortthington and the execution was just two days away. He now had a resigned acceptance to his fate and saw his children for the last time the following day. Like the Tithebarn Street killers, Worthington was Roman Catholic and all three were attended to by Father Bonte, who administered the sacrament early on the morning of the execution.

Worthington went to the scaffold clutching a white handkerchief and was pinioned first by Mr Anderson. Mullen and McCrave were next and the latter, who was described as 'one of the worst type of the dangerous classes' by the *Liverpool Mercury*, showed 'great terror at the hangman's noose'. In contrast his younger friend remained calm throughout. Mr Anderson carried out the execution in a most efficient manner and all three died instantly once the bolt was drawn.

<u>20th April 1875 – Alfred Heap, For the Murder of Margaret McKivett at Manchester</u>

One of the most unusual cases for which somebody was hanged at Kirkdale involved that of Alfred Heap, who was convicted of murder after a botched abortion in Manchester.

Margaret McKivett was a 26 year old single woman who kept a small shop in Hyde Road, Gorton. On Friday 12th March 1875, after discovering she was pregnant, she consulted with Alfred Heap who advertised himself as a surgeon. After having a 2d glass of whiskey in a hotel for courage, she went to Heap's shop where he performed the illegal operation. Whilst this happened, McKivett's mother Sarah Marshall waited in the hotel but when her daughter didn't return she went to see Heap to find out what was going on.

After being met by Heap's housekeeper she was left downstairs but after about two minutes decided to go up anyway. On entering a bedroom she saw Margaret insensible on the bed as Heap tried to revive her with a smelling bottle. Sarah screamed out leading to the housekeeper, named Julia, telling her to shut up so as not to draw attention to the police. Gradually Margaret came round and was taken downstairs by Julia and her mother, while Heap acted totally nonchalantly and went to a nearby beerhouse.

When Margaret began to complain of feeling unwell she asked her mother to fetch Heap, who suggested that all she needed was a nap. A short while later Margaret asked Heap to fetch some whiskey for her and they drank it together, him keeping the change from the sovereign she had given him to pay for it. Two days later Margaret informed her mother that she had miscarried and on the Monday morning Heap was sent for due to her feeling extremely unwell. He was intoxicated when he arrived and first asked if she had had a miscarriage. He then gave her a dose of medicine and said she could have no more until she gave him half a crown.

Sarah refused to do deal with Heap any more and instead arranged for a Dr Fletcher to attend, but Margaret died the following morning. Initially both Heap and Julia Carroll his housekeeper were arrested and charged with murder but ultimately only the case against the doctor was proceeded with. Heap's trial at the Liverpool assizes took place on 2nd April, less than three weeks after Margaret had died. The Crown's position was that even though Heap had not intended to kill, he was still guilty of murder if he had performed an operation that caused injury sufficient enough to bring about a miscarriage. The judge agreed with this, meaning the defence had to try and persuade the jury that the medical evidence was inconclusive. They failed to do so and after being found guilty, there was a strong recommendation for mercy.

Prior to sentencing, Heap told the judge, Baron Pollock, that he was not satisfied with his defence team as they had not called evidence from his wife or her servant. He claimed that Margaret and Sarah had bought tools from his wife to carry out the abortion and that Margaret had been made pregnant by her uncle. Pollock was not impressed by Heap's claims, telling him prior to passing sentence: 'It is quite impossible to suppose that those who were chosen to make the defence for you with every care and ability would deliberately pass over any evidence that could have been the slightest service to you.'

There was then a sensation in the court when Pollock disclosed that Heap had already served a term of five years penal servitude for an offence of this kind and described him as criminal, wretched and wicked. He then passed the death sentence in the usual manner and ignored Heap's request to see his son before being taken to the cells.

4,000 people signed a petition calling for a reprieve and the foreman of the jury came out and said they would have returned a manslaughter verdict if they had known that Heap would hang. The Home Secretary though refused to intervene and Heap soon realised the enormity of the situation he was in. He showed penitence whilst in Kirkdale gaol and listened intently to the sermons of the chaplain. He also wrote a confession to the crime, but denied having had any intent to cause death. He made a lengthy statement which was forwarded by the governor to his son so he could consult with family members over the desirability of publishing it.

On the eve of his execution, which was set for 19th April, Heap retired to bed at midnight. After waking briefly at 3am he slept again and got up at 6am, having a light breakfast and taking Holy Communion. After being pinioned by the executioner William Marwood he walked unaided to the scaffold where he looked up to heaven before the noose was placed around his neck. As soon as he had said 'Lord Jesus receive my soul' the bolt was drawn and death was instantaneous. Over in Manchester, crowds gathered outside Margaret's shop in Hyde Road, which had been closed by her mother who had gone to Southport to keep out of the way. By evening it had grown to several hundred with many beating on the shutters, refusing to believe that Margaret's mother Sarah Marshall wasn't there. Instead they contented themselves with burning an effigy of her.

6th September 1875 – William Baker, For the Murder of Charles Langan at Liverpool & Edward Cooper For the Murder of Edward Jones on the High Seas.

The next double execution at Kirkdale saw pub landlord William Baker killed for shooting a man in one of the most cold blooded killings that had ever been seen in Liverpool. Baker was hanged alongside Edward Cooper, an American seaman who had shot a boatswain at sea.

35 year old William Baker managed the Rainbow in Williamson Square and was the son of a well known and respected victualler in the town. However in the early hours of Sunday 11th July 1875 he got into an altercation at the corner of London Road and St Vincent Street outside the Swan Inn with 34 year old Charles Langan, a cab driver and former prize fighter. The two men had fought the previous year but this time Baker produced a revolver and fired one shot at Langan, who dropped to the ground.

A policeman was on the scene within seconds and was quick to disarm Baker and take him into custody. On arrival at the Bridewell Baker claimed that he was acting in self defence and only intended to hit Langan with the revolver, but it had gone off. Langan was removed to the Royal Infirmary where he was pronounced dead on arrival, the bullet having passed through the base of his skull.

On the Monday at the coroner's inquest witnesses, some of whom knew both men, told how they had been walking up London Road when Baker called out 'Charley I want you'. They went on to say how Langan replied that he had no business with Baker and refused his challenge to a fight. No threats were made before the revolver was produced. The most telling evidence though came from fifteen year old George English, who was returning home from working in a theatre. He didn't know either party but said he was sure he saw Baker fire the shot and there had been no provocation, which helped the jury return a verdict of wilful murder. Baker was committed for trial and on the same day magistrates issued warrants for the arrests of two men who had threatened prosecution witnesses.

The trial at the assizes took place on 17th August, with witnesses giving consistent evidence in relation to the way the shot was fired. Baker claimed that he bought the revolver to defend himself as he had been threatened by Langan previously, but couldn't show that he had been provoked immediately prior to the shooting. In summing up, Mr Justice Archibald said that there was no doubt about whether or not Baker had carried out the shooting, the only question was as to whether he had intended the gun to go off. If the jury believed that he hadn't then a verdict of manslaughter could be returned.

After retiring for an hour and a half, a guilty verdict was returned with a recommendation for mercy. Prior to receiving the death sentence, Baker told the court that his counsel had adopted the wrong line of defence and that the jury should have learnt more about Langan's character. As he donned the black cap, Justice Archibald said he had acted in the most wanton manner and he would have been astonished if the jury had reached any other conclusion.

Baker, who was married with a young child, had a lot of friends in Liverpool and with his father being a well known tradesman there was plenty of sympathy on his part. However he was also a known local rough, having previously been convicted of assault and robbery. A petition was presented to the Home Secretary, signed by eleven of the jury and ten town councillors. This was met with an angry response by Langan's brothers, who objected to claims that he had threatened Baker after being refused service in the Rainbow. On 4th September, three days before the execution date, the Home Secretary confirmed there would be no reprieve.

Baker awaited his fate along with Edward Cooper, who was the first American to be executed at Kirkdale. He was 33 years old and from New Orleans, although had been at sea since he was in his teens and usually worked on ships owned by Messrs Ferguson of South Castle Street in Liverpool. It was there in January 1875 that he registered to work on the *Coldbeck*, which was undertaking a voyage to Valpairaiso in Chile.

On 24th April in the early evening the *Coldbeck* was near Cape Horn when Edward Jones, the boatswain, went to the forecastle and ordered Cooper to help put up one of the sails. Cooper refused, saying he was drinking tea and when Jones told him again, he produced a revolver. Jones told him to put it down and fight like a man on the deck, but Cooper responded by shooting him in the chest in front of another seaman and went to his bunk. Other sailors raced to the forecastle, where Jones was bleeding heavily and saying 'Lord have mercy on my soul, I am done for.' He was carried to his cabin but soon died and Cooper was placed in chains by the captain, responding by saying the shooting was inevitable once Jones was put in charge.

The *Coldbeck* continued its voyage to Valpairaiso where the revolver was placed in a sealed package by the British consul. Cooper was then brought back aboard the *Iberian*, which arrived in Liverpool on 23rd July. He was handed over to the river police by Captain Brown and appeared in the police court that afternoon, where he was remanded for a week. The following Friday he reappeared at the police court where he was committed to trial at the assizes.

Cooper stood trial on 14th August, with the *Liverpool Mercury* describing him as 'of intelligent appearance.' The jury heard how he was of good character and had never caused any of his captains any trouble before. However fellow seamen gave evidence that the orders which were given to him were to be expected and not done so in unreasonable manner. As such

Cooper's claim that he acted in self defence was not upheld and he was found guilty of murder, but with a recommendation of mercy. He showed no emotion as he was sentenced to death and was then taken to Kirkdale gaol.

Whilst in gaol, Cooper received very few visitors, being a single man with no family or friends in Liverpool. One of his visitors was a passenger who was on the *Iberian* that brought him back to England. Unable to read or write, he had never heard of the Lord's Prayer but turned to Catholicism whilst in the condemned cell, regularly being attended to by Father Bonte. The Sailors' Home petitioned the Home Secretary for his reprieve, but Cooper himself didn't hold out much hope and his only wish was that he could be shot instead of hanged. He received confirmation that there would be no reprieve the same day as Baker on 4th September, with both now set to hang two days later.

Whereas Cooper remained relatively calm in the days leading to the execution Baker was the complete opposite, often breaking down completely and begging for divine mercy. On the night before the execution he didn't sleep at all whereas Cooper slept soundly. Both men got up soon after 5am and had breakfast before being attended to by their respective chaplains, Baker being a Protestant and Cooper a Catholic.

The procession to the scaffold started at two minutes past eight. The *Liverpool Mercury* reported that Baker had to be helped up and looked 'bewildered, haggard and pale', unlike Cooper who went 'nobly to the scaffold.' After the rope was placed around Baker's neck he closed his eyes and never opened them again, but Cooper remained calm and said to those present: 'All that I can say gentlemen is that I have not had justice.' Both fervently repeated their chaplains' prayers and when the bolt was drawn they dropped to an instant death, the press reporting that there were no tremors and convulsions. The executioner Marwood had done his job well, with the Mercury reporting the next day that Cooper even had a slight smile on his face.

Outside the gaol there were hundreds of people, most of them sympathisers of Baker who went away after the black flag was hoisted. As a mark of respect, the Rainbow remained closed all day while the blinds in his father's premises next door remained drawn.

The next execution at Kirkdale was also a double one involving Everton man Richard Thompson who was hanged for killing his girlfriend's landlord who objected to his visits. He was hanged alongside William Fish, a barber from Blackburn who had been responsible for a brutal child murder.

Thompson, a 22 year old labourer, was courting a lady named Mary Corfield who lodged with John Blundell and his wife in Haigh Street. Blundell wasn't happy about the two of them often being alone in the parlour and expressed his dissatisfaction at this, but as Thompson had been best man at his wedding four months earlier there was little expectation that the situation would deteriorate so much. Things came to a head on 14th April 1876 when Thompson walked past and saw Blundell's wife Margaret on the step. He swung his belt and shouted at her 'Send him out and I will put him in his coffin before the night is over.'

The following evening, Blundell was helping Mary's brother William move house and was carrying a box down nearby Coronation Street. They came across Thompson who immediately acted with a threatening demeanour, and after Blundell asked 'What's to do with you Dick' he was grabbed around the neck. Thompson then took an open knife out of his pocket and stabbed Blundell up to twelve times. Blundell was taken home but as he was bleeding heavily he was admitted to the Workhouse Hospital, where he died on 17th April at around 10pm. Around four hours before Blundell passed away, Thompson had handed himself in to the Rose Hill Bridewell, having been on the run since the stabbing.

Whilst close to the point of death 23 year old Blundell had told the chaplain Reverend Ebenezer Smith that he 'freely forgave

Thompson'. His condition had deteriorated quite quickly and a magistrate sent to take a deposition didn't get there in time. However, the evidence of William Corfield and a boy who was shown a knife by Thompson earlier in the evening but told not to worry as it was for someone else, was enough for the inquest to return a verdict of wilful murder. He was then committed to the assizes on a coroner's warrant and listed to appear before Mr Justice Lindley on 29th July.

There was little doubt that Thompson had carried out the stabbing, the only issue was whether it was manslaughter or murder. In summing up, the judge said that if there had been no provocation then the jury had to return a verdict of murder, even if there had been no intent to kill. It took ten minutes for them to find Thompson guilty and he said 'I would liked to have seen my witnesses he threatened to lay me out.' Justice Lindley said that death had resulted from 'too free use of the knife' before donning the black cap and passing sentence. Thompson, who had remained calm throughout the trial, then burst into tears before being taken to the cells.

Whereas Thompson's killing of Blundell was somewhat ordinary the killing of seven year old Emily Holland by William Fish at Blackburn was the complete opposite. The *Liverpool Mercury* said that it was 'unparalleled in its hideous details' the day after the execution and at the trial the paper felt that 'in the annals of our criminal jurisprudence no such terrible indictment had ever been presented in court.' The last time Emily was seen alive was at 415pm on 28th March 1876 when she bought some tobacco at Cox's confectioners shop in Moss Street on her way home from school. The shop was just a stone's throw from her home but she never made it there and her anxious parents notified the police of her disappearance. Then on the morning of 30th March there was a tragic discovery when various parts of her body, but not the arms or head, were found in a field and drains outside the town on Whalley Old Road.

It was suspected that Emily had bought the tobacco for a barber and 26 year old Fish fitted the description of a man who she had pointed out to her friend as getting it for. He had a shop further down Moss Street, just thirty yards away and lived with his family in another house in the street. However he managed to display psychopathic tendencies when questioned by the police, calmly pointing to his own circumstances as a father of two young children and offering to assist the many other volunteers who were desperate to find the killer. On the day of Emily's funeral the procession passed his shop and he sat in the window calmly smoking his pipe and watching it go past.

Fish was finally arrested thanks to a painter from Preston who offered the services of his bloodhound, Morgan. On 16th April the dog was taken to the place where the torso was found and then to his shop where it first smelt in the kitchen then took detectives upstairs and stopped at the fireplace. An officer put his hand up the chimney and discovered parts of a child's skull which had some hairs attached. After being arrested Fish stood firm and said he had no idea how the bones had got there. Word soon got round and police had great difficulty removing him to the lock up due to baying crowds wanting to lynch him.

A further search of Fish's shop the following day uncovered parts of clothing that matched what was found in the field. When confronted with this new evidence he made a full confession saying he had induced Emily to go upstairs and raped her before cutting her throat. He then took the body downstairs and dismembered it before wrapping the parts in newspaper and dumping them, then reopened the shop and shaved some customers. After making the confession Fish was visited by his wife who told him she forgave him but that he should now prepare himself for another world.

The previously adjourned coroner's inquest took place on 20th April at the assembly room of Blackburn Town Hall. A crucial witness was a boy who said the shutters of the shop were unusually down when he went there for a haircut shortly after Emily had last been seen. Fish's written confession was read out and the jury returned a verdict of wilful murder against him, meaning he was committed for trial at the Liverpool assizes. A tramp named Taylor, who had been arrested a week earlier on the basis of having been seen near Cox's confectionery shop on the afternoon of the disappearance, was then discharged in a state of bewilderment. Outside the court he was hoisted shoulder high by the crowd and given several offers of food and drink.

Despite the trial taking place at St George's Hall in Liverpool on 28th July, hundreds of people from Blackburn weren't deterred from attending. Special trains were laid on and extra police had to be drafted in to keep those without tickets from forcing their way into the building. Fish was pale and frightened as he was brought up from the cells. Even though he had confessed he pleaded not guilty and this led to Emily's mother and father, described in the *Liverpool Mercury* as 'most respectable people' having to give evidence. Her mother broke down when asked to identify some of the hair retrieved from the skull found at Fish's shop as that of her missing daughter.

Fish's only hope of avoiding the death penalty was if his defence counsel could prove that the act happened in a period of temporary insanity. However Dr Martland, who examined him on the day of his arrest and trial, said he 'showed not the slightest symptoms of lunacy' and was 'not suffering from a fit of mania' at the time of the murder. Judge Lindley summed up telling the jury that if they felt Fish's confession fitted with the other facts of the case then he was guilty of murder. It took less than a minute for the jury to return this verdict and when asked if he had anything to say Fish replied that at the time of the killing he didn't know what he was doing. The judge wasted few words on him saying simply: 'You have been found guilty of this murder and for this murder you must die' before passing sentence in the usual manner.

At Kirkdale gaol Fish showed much penitence and was visited daily by the chaplain Octavius Pigott. He prayed fervently and knowing the hopelessness of his position, prepared solely for life in the next world. He was a gently spoken prisoner and one of the warders commented to the press that it was hard to believe he was responsible for 'one of the most diabolical outrages of modern times.' He wrote to his wife saying that he did not know what he was doing and God would be his judge. Even when he sent Emily to the shop for tobacco, he wrote that killing her was not then in his mind.

Fish's relatives visited him for the last time on 10th August, with quite a large crowd coming from Blackburn simply to see his family members go through the gaol gates. He was visited by his wife, two children, mother, uncle and brother in law. His children did not seem to understand what was going on with his two year old daughter saying 'What are you crying for mamma' as they left. After showing a resigned acceptance following their departure he devoted the rest of his time to prayer and also wrote an open letter. This urged people to go to Sunday school, as it was leaving there that led to his bad ways.

Whereas Fish knew he had no chance of a reprieve Thompson was hopeful. His solicitor Frederick Ponton of Vernon Chambers in Dale Street fought hard but on 12th August the Home Secretary wrote to him saying he could see no grounds for granting one. He remained indifferent to his fate, taking little notice of the chaplain and not requesting a final visit from his mother, who he had last seen on 7th August. Instead he remained satisfied that he would receive divine forgiveness as his victim had forgiven him.

The two prisoners last day on earth was warm and sunny, but the following morning they woke to an autumnal mist. Fish had spent an extremely restless night and refused breakfast, but Thompson did partake of a little food. At 7am they received the Holy Communion with Thompson paying much more attention to the chaplain than previously.

The press were admitted at 745am, with procedures having been tightened so that nobody was admitted unless they had a document signed by the chairman of the visiting justices. At 8am the pinioning was complete and the procession to the scaffold began. Fish was accompanied by Reverend George Hays of Blackburn whilst Octavius Pigott, the goal chaplain, walked alongside Thompson. Fish was in a state of bewilderment and recited prayers repeatedly, but in contrast Thompson had a wry smile.

As Thompson was having the rope put around his neck Fish started to stumble and had to be held up by two warders. Thompson was crying and singing 'Safe in the Arms of Jesus' as the final preparations were made, then the bolt was drawn and both dropped with great force and died instantly, Marwood again having calculated everything perfectly. The *Liverpool Mercury* reported that both bodies showed signs of a fast violent death, Fish's cheeks having red patches on them.

Outside the gaol hundreds had gathered, many expressing dissatisfaction at hangings now taking place in private. One sailor on his way to the docks enquired as to why so many people were about and was told 'only two men hung.' Many labourers working at nearby brickfields downed tools and came over when the prison bell tolled. After the execution the black flag was raised and a few minutes later a group of excursionists arrived from Blackburn, showing disappointment that they were too late to see the spectacle.

After being cut down the bodies were laid out in a storeroom for the inquest to take place. Once this was complete they were placed in simple coffins and carried by other prisoners to the corner of the gaol where burials took place. A phrenologist was allowed to take a cast of Fish's head for further examination. Particular interest had been shown into Fish's state of mind as his father had been jailed for neglect of his children and as an eleven year old he had fallen forty feet from a bridge and been epileptic ever since.

<u>12th February 1878 – James Trickett, For the Murder of Mary Trickett at Liverpool</u>

The first single hanging at Kirkdale in almost three years was that of a pest control worker who had killed his wife, claiming it was as a result of her drunkenness.

James Trickett was 42 years old and lived with his wife Mary and two young children in Hopwood Street, Vauxhall. He worked as a freelance rat catcher, regularly being employed by the corporation, dock board and large mercantile firms. He was also known as a bird fancier, having a number of cages in his house and yard from where he also sold seeds.

At around 8pm on 26th December 1877 a neighbour Margaret Brown heard screams coming from inside Trickett's property and looked through the window, where she saw Trickett kicking at his wife. A boy was screaming 'Please come to bed mother.' After discretely waiting around Margaret saw Mary get up and sit on a chair, before going upstairs. She then heard Mary scream again and her husband shouting 'Is this not a nice bed for a man to lie on.'

Demetrius Caralli, a carter who lived opposite also heard some of the commotion but was so used to it he did not investigate any further. Trickett's son went over and asked for help but he would not intervene. A few moments later Trickett came out looking wild and with bloodied hands, went into a herbalists shop next door and said 'It is done.' He then returned home and put the shutters up. A flatman named John Shore who was returning to his home two doors away was passing Trickett's house when he appeared and said 'Come in John I have killed the wife'. John went upstairs and saw Mary lying semi conscious on the floor with a knife next to her, although there was no blood.

In desperation, Trickett's son went to Susannah Bowen's house at the corner of Hopwood Street and Latimer Street, saying to her 'For God's sake please come and see if you can help me.' Susannah did go there and found Trickett bathing Mary's forehead with a sponge and he asked her to send for Father Duggan. Susannah replied that a doctor was needed too and when asked by Trickett to lie for him and say she had fallen down the stairs and hit her head on a box, she said she could not do so.

It did not take long for the police to become aware that something was wrong and at 830pm Inspector Donaldson arrived, by which time Mary had passed away. Trickett was still bathing her head and said she had fallen down the stairs, but the officer noticed there was now a large amount of blood on the floor and bedclothes. Inspector Donaldson made a brief search of the house and could find no murder weapon, but he did notice there was no blood on the stairs which would have been the case if Trickett's version of events was true. As he was taken into custody Trickett said: 'God knows I love her but if I am going to be hung for it so be it, she has been drunk for the last 31 weeks.'

As Trickett was being taken to the Main Bridewell he fainted twice. Constable Grayson made a more thorough search of the bedroom and found two parts of a broken stick, one of them having blood at the end of it. The doctor who carried out the post mortem found wounds on the cheek and forehead, of the size that could have been caused by the stick that Grayson had found. A six inch wound was found in the body which had penetrated the liver and was believed to have been caused by a knife. On 29th December an inquest revealed that Mary was in the advanced stages of pregnancy and returned a verdict of wilful murder against her husband.

At the assizes on 24th January 1878 Trickett pleaded 'not guilty' firmly and gave a military salute. Neighbours gave evidence and Dr Costine said there was no way the wound in the body could have been caused by falling on a box. Trickett's defence said that there was no aforethought or malice and that instead he should be found guilty of manslaughter, albeit of the worst kind. After fifteen minutes deliberation the jury asked for clarification as to whether any of Mary's clothing had been penetrated during the stabbing. Dr Costine produced her gown and chemise, both of which had been cut and after another fifteen minutes a verdict of guilty of murder was returned, with a strong recommendation for mercy on account of the provocation received.

When asked by Baron Pollock if he had anything to say, Trickett gave quite a lengthy statement, saying that on returning home that evening he found his wife in a drunken condition and as he was preparing his supper and lighting a fire, she fell off the stool and cut her head. He finished it by saying: 'When my wife was sober I had a heaven of a home with my meals regular and rooms clean, but when she turned to drink it was the opposite way.' Baron Pollock though dismissed this statement saying he was at a loss as to how Trickett thought this explanation of her death could be believed given the evidence. Telling him he was supposed to be his wife's 'natural protector' but had instead gave 'considerable brutality' the judge passed the death sentence and as he was removed to the cells Trickett waved to somebody.

While awaiting his fate at Kirkdale Trickett was regularly attended to by Father Bonte and showed great penitence. He was told on Saturday 9th February that the Home Secretary could find no grounds to commute the sentence, having received an appeal by his solicitor Mr Ponton of Vernon Chambers. He had held high hopes of a reprieve but after hearing he would be hanged simply said 'thy will be done.' His main concern was that his children would not have to enter the workhouse and he was comforted by the knowledge that his brother and wife had agreed to raise them. There were tear jerking scenes later that day when they made a last visit to him. He also asked that reporters be aware he was dying on behalf of his wife and had no bad feeling against anyone.

With Marwood being double booked and required in Winchester, this execution took place on a Tuesday instead of the usual Monday. It was a bright and sunny, albeit cold morning and when Marwood checked the apparatus he lifted his hat and cheerily said 'Good morning' to the assembled journalists. Shortly before 8am the solemn procession began with Father Bonte chanting the litany for the dying. Trickett walked firmly with two warders either side and the governor Major Leggett behind him. He showed no emotion and said nothing as he stepped onto the scaffold and had his legs strapped and the hood placed over his head. The noose was placed around his neck and the bolt drawn, death occurring instantly.

18th May 1879 – Thomas Johnson, For the Murder of Eliza Patten at Liverpool

The hanging of Thomas Johnson for the murder of a woman he was in a relationship with was the first to which the press were not admitted. Described as 'one of the terrible phases of depravity that exists amongst us' by the *Liverpool Mercury*, 21 year old Johnson took the reasons for the killing with him to the next world.

Johnson had been seeing Eliza Patten, who was also 21 and described by the papers as an 'Unfortunate' for about two years. They occasionally stayed at lodging houses in the Dingle area and for reasons that were never fully explained, were told to leave one at 59 Prince William Street on Saturday 22nd March 1879. After spending an uncomfortable night nearby, Eliza went to a 'house of ill fame' next door to their previous lodgings and asked to be allowed to cook some breakfast for 'Demon', as Johnson was known. He was one of the notorious 'cornermen' that plagued Liverpool's streets and had been imprisoned before for stealing rope and being a vagabond.

After having bacon and eggs Johnson sent out for some beer and the couple spent the afternoon drinking with some other residents. With chairs at a premium, Johnson sat on the floor by the fire with Eliza resting her head on his lap. Mrs McCannon who kept the house allowed them to take a room and they then went upstairs to rest at about 5pm, having had very little sleep the night before. Rather than sleep though there was an argument and Johnson came downstairs saying he needed a pipe for Eliza. She followed him and it was seen by Mrs McCannon that there was a cut on her head, which she said had been caused by a candlestick. Without explanation or warning, Johnson then took a knife out of a canister and stabbed Eliza behind the ear whilst the others were watching, then ran out and off in the direction of the river.

Mrs McCannon's husband, who was about to leave for Widnes where he worked during the week, called for a policeman and Eliza was removed to the Southern Hospital. She died soon afterwards, a post mortem establishing that the jugular vein had been severed. Johnson had managed to escape over to Rock Ferry but the following evening he was back in Liverpool and apprehended by police in an empty house in Upper Mann Street. On being taken into custody he said: 'Alright I did it but I did not intend to kill her.' An inquest was held on 26th March at which Eliza's father explained how he had not seen his daughter for five years, even though the family home was nearby in Hampton Street. After a verdict of wilful murder was returned Johnson was committed for trial.

Johnson appeared at the Liverpool assizes on 9th May, where witnesses who saw the assault gave evidence in addition to some other 'unfortunates' who he had discussed the event with in the aftermath. He had told them that he did it after being struck by the candlestick, but wouldn't say what the row was over in the first place. The surgeon who carried out the post mortem said that the depth of Eliza's wound indicated the blow had been struck with considerable force. However his defence counsel suggested a manslaughter verdict was more appropriate given the killing had taken place in the heat of the moment. The judge did not do him many favours in summing up though, pointing out that sufficient time had passed between him being hit by the candlestick upstairs and the stabbing, which occurred when he was not under threat.

It took the jury just two minutes to find Johnson guilty of murder. After having presented an air of indifference during the trial and earlier proceedings, he broke down crying and had to be carried downstairs by the warders. At Kirkdale he was attended to by Father Bonte and showed great penitence, but held out little hope of a reprieve and continued to withhold the reasons behind the killing. He was visited by his sister who travelled from

America on hearing of his arrest, the parting scene being described as a 'breast rending one'. Johnson was scheduled to be executed alongside Emily Jones, a 20 year old laundress who had killed her illegitimate child, but with just a day to spare her sentence was commuted to life imprisonment.

A small crowd of labourers gathered outside the gaol at 8am on the morning of 28th May and they were joined by a number of journalists. For the first time the press had been refused entry due to new national regulations but were but told they could attend the inquest. After the black flag was hoisted the crowd remained for an hour, hoping to get a glimpse of the executioner Marwood but he was instead ushered out of a side door. When journalists were allowed into the inquest they were barred from viewing he body, but prison officials did share news of the execution itself. They advised how Johnson had ate a light breakfast and gone firmly to the scaffold whilst shedding a few tears. Death, they said, was instantaneous.

The murder for which Patrick Kearns and Hugh Burns were hanged was one that created great excitement throughout the whole of England and not just Lancashire. They and Mary Tracey, who was later respited, were convicted purely on circumstantial evidence but the chain of events left no doubt of their guilt. When the trio were sentenced for killing Mary's husband Patrick Tracey, the trial judge described the case as 'from the basest and wickedest of all base and wicked motives'

In the early hours of 24th October 1879 screams were heard from a house in 60 Oxford Street, Widnes. Neighbours went to investigate and found Patrick Tracey, a 36 year old labourer at Muspratt's chemical works, had been shot dead. His much younger wife Mary and lodgers Kearns and Burns said that a burglar had stolen £15 from a box downstairs before going upstairs and shooting Patrick as he lay beside his wife and child.

The police were sceptical of this version of events though. It seemed inconceivable that a burglar would enter a property, steal what he needed then go upstairs and shoot just one resident of the house. Cobwebs and dirt by the window where the thief had supposedly entered was undisturbed and there was no blood on Mary's clothing, even though she was supposed to have been in bed next to her husband at the time. When Kearns and Burns expressed a desire to go to work at 4am, officers acted fast and took them into custody where they remained whilst further enquiries took place.

When statements were obtained from neighbours it became apparent that there was friction between husband and wife, while Mary was enjoying greater intimacy with 24 year old Kearns than she ought to have been. It was also discovered that over the previous year Patrick's life had been insured to the total sum of £350, seven times his annual salary. Mary had also attempted to take out a policy worth £100 in her husbands name without his knowledge, but the agent declined to accept it given his high level of cover elsewhere. It was established that Mary had financial problems, owing sums to a number of tradesmen and had been borrowing money, yet she claimed to have had £15 locked away in a box doing nothing. The motive was clear and police soon discovered that there was the means to do it as well when Burns and Kearns were found to have bought a pistol and ammunition shortly before the murder.

There was finally enough evidence to hold an inquest at the Grosvenor hotel on 13th November. The jury returned a verdict of wilful murder against Kearns and Burns, as well as Mary who was immediately taken into custody. The following day at the police court they were committed to trial at the Liverpool assizes and taken to Kirkdale gaol. In an attempt to save his own life, Kearns wrote to Inspector Barnett at Widnes police station on 24th January asking to see him immediately. Three days later the inspector arrived and took a lengthy statement from Kearns, who claimed he had been asleep at the time and was woken by the screams and then got up to find thirty year old Burns and Mary outside the bedroom with Patrick dead inside. He went on to say that after he suspected all was not as it seemed Burns threatened him with a pistol saying he would be shot too if he didn't keep his mouth shut. Inspector Barnett was confident though that there was evidence to convict all three accused and did not see the need for one of them to turn Queen's evidence.

Mary was heavily pregnant by the time the trial arrived and throughout it would often stand up and clutch the rails of the dock, exhibiting signs of intense pain. It took a lengthy two days (12th and 13th February) with the prosecution going over all the pieces of evidence to ensure they fitted together to implicate all three. They were found guilty after just twenty minutes deliberation by the jury and Lord Coleridge delivered his damning assessment of their character, saying that their wickedest and basest act had been carried out on a 'harmless and unoffending man.' Telling them to prepare to stand before God he said that his 'wisdom is infinite and mercy unspeakable.' After an appeal by defence counsel Dr Cummins, Lord Coleridge immediately respited Mary's execution until after she had given birth. The 28 year old already had three other children who were all aged under five, two of whom were taken back to Ireland by her father and the other given to a family in Oxford Street.

Like Mary, Kearns and Burns were from Ireland and had come to Widnes about three years earlier to seek work as labourers. At Kirkdale gaol they were attended to by Father Bonte and both received visits from family members, Burns's sister seeing him the day before his execution. Once again the press were not admitted and had to remain outside the gaol on the morning of 2nd March along with a solitary policeman and around 100 men who braved the cold despite two inches of snow falling. One man had come from Ireland with the hope of seeing Kearns but he was refused admission. There were also a small number of interested onlookers who had travelled from Widnes.

The execution was delayed a short while due to the late arrival of the High Sheriff of Lancashire who first went to Walton gaol by mistake. The cab taking him to Kirkdale then damaged a wheel which needed replacing, meaning it was 817am before the black flag was hoisted to confirm that it had taken place. The journalists were then allowed inside to attend the inquest, where it was established that death was instant in both cases. Unlike the previous occasion though, prison warders were less willing to pass any details of the actual execution to them.

Mary remained in Kirkdale gaol and was visited by her brother a few days later. On 13th March, exactly one month after she was sentenced, she received communication from the Home Office that her sentence had been commuted to penal servitude for life. She was then transferred to Woking in Surrey.

The murder for which 52 year old William Turner was hanged was an all too familiar case of an attack by a husband on his wife whilst under the influence of drink. Turner was angry that his wife felt unwell and wanted to return home from a public house, leading to him kicking her to death.

On the evening of Friday 23rd June the couple went to the Sinkers Arms beerhouse in Sandy Lane, Skelmersdale but after one glass of beer Ellen said she felt unwell with a cold. William refused to take her home and instead bought more ale but after further pleas he agreed to do so. He was clearly not happy about this, as he continued to act in a threatening manner to 65 year old Ellen, who was generally healthy apart from a club foot. That evening though she felt so bad that another customer Joseph Jones loaned a cart for her to be wheeled back.

Both Turner and Ellen were in the cart which was wheeled back by Jones, who heard him say to her 'I'll kill you tonight.' When they got to their home at Black Moss Cottages, a neighbour Elizabeth Lindsay helped Turner get Ellen inside. She then sat on a chair but fell onto the floor whilst her husband was sat on the sofa. Inexplicably, Turner got up and put his boots on and said 'I'll be hung for thy sake before morning' before kicking her all over her body. A woman in the house said 'How can you do that to an old woman' and Turner replied that he would do the same to her. When she stepped in between them she received a kick in the leg. The assault only stopped when Ellen pleaded that she was almost killed.

Ellen's body was found to be a mass of bruises when Mrs Lindsay undressed and washed her on the Sunday morning, when Turner was not present. She called a doctor who examined her and found a fractured shoulder and severe bruising to the eye, hip, right arm and private parts. Dr Dumbreck continued to attend and was with Ellen when she died on 27th June, a post mortem determining the cause as shock to the system due to her injuries. The inquest two days later returned a verdict of wilful murder and on 30th June Turner appeared at Ormskirk Magistrates' Court where he was committed to the next assizes at Liverpool.

On 3rd August Turner was tried before Mr Justice North. When Mrs Lindsay gave her evidence, there were gasps as she said Turner could not have kicked any harder if he was kicking at a boulder stone. Dr Dumbreck said that although there was some kidney disease and fatty degeneration around the heart, they were not serious enough to cause death, which was instead as a direct result of the violence she had received. This was disputed by Turner's defence counsel, but the jury took just ten minutes to return a guilty verdict. Justice North said he had no doubt about the correctness of the verdict and passed the death sentence, Turner showing no emotion at all.

Whilst awaiting trial Turner had shown a complete ignorance to religious matters but his attitude changed once he was under the sentence of death. The gaol chaplain Octavius Pigott was formerly based in a mining district so Turner had some affinity with him. He also welcomed the attentions of a Mr Pearson, who was engaged by the governor to read scriptures to him. Turner made no attempt to get a reprieve and never denied his guilt. He told officials he bitterly regretted his wife's death, believing she was sitting there sulking and not saying anything to him.

Two of his sisters, described as being 'of the artisan class' visited him for the last time on 19th August but former colliery mates were not allowed in by the gaol. On the day before his execution he visited the chapel twice and went to bed early, sleeping quite soundly. After rising at 6am he took Holy Communion at the chapel and was then taken to the pinioning room where the process was done with speed and efficiency.

The executioner William Marwood had been at Kirkdale since the Saturday night, staying at a nearby hotel.

An application for the press to witness the execution was refused by the High Sheriff, meaning that between 7 and 8am journalists mingled with the small crowd outside the gaol gates. A few minutes before 8am the bell tolled and soon afterwards those near the wall heard a thud, which was believed to be the drop. Just after this the black flag was hoisted. An hour later the inquest took place which heard that death had been instant, and one warder said that Turner had walked more steadily to his execution than any other man he had seen.

4th December 1882 - Bernard Mullarkey, For the Murder of Thomas Cruse at Maghull

Bernard Mullarkey became the first teenager to be hanged at Kirkdale since McCrave and Mullen in 1875, having been convicted on entirely circumstantial evidence of the murder of two men by setting fire to a farm building.

Originally from County Mayo in Ireland, Mullarkey came to England in 1879 at the age of 16. He had a brief spell in the army with the 95th Regiment of Foot, from which he deserted, before taking a series of labouring jobs and eventually ending up in Maghull where he worked for a farmer named John Sumner.

Mullarkey slept in an outhouse on the farm with three other workers - a father and son both named Thomas Cruse and a man named Thomas Jordan. There appeared to be no ill feeling between them at first but during the month of September 1882 Mullarkey's attitude began to change. On 23rd September he was in Culshaw's beerhouse and shouted out 'You lot are playing the monkey on me but I'll play it on them I'll swing for young Cruse and set fire to the place.'

Just two days after the outburst in the beerhouse, all four men went to Bradley's provisions shop in the evening and on returning to the farm, Mullarkey told the others he was going to the washhouse and they went to sleep in the loft. Soon afterwards though, one of the men was awoken by screams and saw that the barn was alight. As they desperately tried to put the flames out with sacks, one of them looked out of the window to see Mullarkey standing in a courtyard, having got the horses out of danger. Rather than get a nearby ladder to help, Mullarkey instead went away to find Mr Sumner and by the time he arrived back one of the three men, the elder Thomas Cruse, was dead.

After putting out the flames a police sergeant who arrived on the scene asked Mullarkey what he knew. Giving his name as

Charles Rogers, he said that he had fallen asleep drunk in the washhouse and woke to find the building on fire, having no idea how it had started. The policeman was able to establish that the fire had been started from below the loft, indicating that none of the three men in there could have been responsible. Mr Cruse's body was also found to have received a blow to the head before the fire had started, leading to Mullarkey's arrest on 28th September.

An inquest returned a verdict of wilful murder and Mullarkey was committed for a trial that took place at Liverpool Assizes on 17th November. The evidence against him was largely circumstantial as nobody had seen him start the fire or enter the outhouse. However, in summing up, Justice Day pointed to the threats made a few days before, his odd behaviour at the time of the fire and the fact that those giving evidence as to his conduct had no reason to lie. Damningly, he also said that if Mullarkey set fire to the building knowing somebody was inside then it was murder.

The jury took just seventeen minutes to return a verdict of guilty and Justice Day said that this verdict had been reached 'on evidence that must have carried conviction to the mind of every person who heard it.' After being sentenced to death, Mullarkey replied: 'Well sir, you can only judge a fellow on this earth. You can not judge me in the next, where we shall all be judged. I am as innocent of the crime I am going to swing for as the child who is not born yet. I am going before my God now.'

Despite his rather uncooperative past Mullarkey showed the greatest respect to Major Leggett at Kirkdale as well as the other prison officials. He also paid careful attention to the words of Father Bonte. He was visited by two cousins, but he refused to allow his parents to spend what little money they had on coming to see him. In his final letter to them he wrote that he had been an indifferent son, but his life had been 'a short and merry one.'

Mullarkey twice attended divine service on the day before his execution and slept soundly. He then got up at 6am, had a good breakfast and had the last sacrament administered by Father Bonte. Again journalists were not allowed into the execution and they waited outside as William Marwood completed the process swiftly and humanely. The black flag was then hoisted and after hanging for an hour Mullarkey's body was cut down and the press were allowed in to observe the formalities of the inquest.

3rd December 1883 – Charles Dutton, For the Murder of Hannah Hamshaw at Liverpool

Charles Dutton was another murderer whose crime had no motive and was carried out in a drunken rage. He had killed his wife's grandmother after the couple had had an argument earlier in the day and his execution did not go as smoothly as others had in recent years.

Hannah Hamshaw was a seventy year old widow living at 160 Athol Street in Vauxhall with her granddaughter Charlotte and her husband Charles Dutton, a 23 year old driller who was commonly known by his middle name of Harry. The couple had been married in May 1883, with Dutton showing violent tendencies on the occasional times he drank to excess.

On the afternoon of 6th October that year Charlotte was at her friend Harriet Kay's home at St Martin's Cottages in Silvester Street. Dutton arrived, having clearly been drinking and some words were exchanged between him and Charlotte, who then left with him. Twenty minutes later they returned and Dutton attempted to strike his wife but Harriet intervened, telling him to leave the property. He did so but Charlotte went with him and Harriet followed them to Athol Street, observing him making threats all the way.

Later in the evening Dutton knocked at Harriet's home asking if Charlotte was there, saying they had had words over tea and she had ran out. Harriet replied she had not seen her and he replied that he would 'do for one of them tonight' and went to a public house in Athol Street. At around 11pm Harriet went to fetch Charlotte and took her to St Martin's Cottages for her own safety. After midnight, Harriet's husband James went to check on Hannah, but Dutton refused to open the door claiming that there was a mob there as well who were after him.

Knowing something was not right James sought the help of other neighbours and forced entry through the back, finding Hannah sitting down and bleeding heavily. A doctor was called but on his arrival Hannah was quite insensible and lived for only another ten minutes. There were wounds all over her face and upper body, which he concluded had been brought about by considerable violence.

Dutton had made his escape and went to a friend Joseph Whitehead's house in Tindall Street, where he had earlier been and said he would be locking his wife out as she was seeing another man. Dutton produced a set of keys and said he was satisfied, leading to Joseph going to the police and he was subsequently apprehended whilst hiding under the stairs. On being searched, the keys, a razor blade and knife were found on Dutton's possession and he claimed that all he had done was push the old woman and left her sitting there alive.

At the inquest on 9th October three neighbours said that they had heard screams coming from Hannah's house, one of them saying they heard shouts of 'Oh Harry don't.' Another had been confronted by an angry Dutton asking where his wife was and when she said she didn't know he threatened 'to do for her.' The jury took only a few minutes to return a verdict of wilful murder and commended the conduct of Mr and Mrs Kay.

Dutton was then committed to trial at the next assizes, where he appeared before Mr Justice Denman on 17th November. There was a brief delay when a juror asked to be discharged as a conscientious objector because he didn't want to find a man guilty if it meant a death sentence. This was agreed to and another sworn in, then Mr and Mrs Kay gave their evidence, along with other neighbours from Athol Street. One of them had heard Dutton shout 'Tell me where my wife is or I'll do your entails in' while another told how Dutton had asked to swap jackets in Tindall Street. The doctor who had attended that night reconfirmed his opinion from the inquest, saying that the injuries were inconsistent with a fall and that Hannah was otherwise healthy.

The defence counsel acknowledged that Dutton had carried out the killing, but said that there had been no intent to kill and that it had occurred in a fit of mental aberration, meaning manslaughter was more appropriate. The jury though disagreed, finding Dutton guilty of murder following half an hour's deliberation. Asked if he had anything to say, Dutton repeated what he had said on arrest, that he had simply pushed Hannah backwards after she said she didn't know where his wife was. Justice Denman made it clear he had no qualms with the verdict, telling him prior to sentence: 'If the jury had not found you guilty of that crime upon such evidence as what was given it would have been a great misfortune for the inhabitants of this country.' Dutton then showed no emotion as the death sentence was passed in the usual form.

At Kirkdale Dutton was attended to by gaol chaplain Octavius Pigott and listened intently. He urged the reverend to pass on to people that they should be wary of hasty marital contracts, evil tempers and drunkenness. On 2nd December, the day before the execution, he finally admitted full responsibility for the death and retired to bed late but still slept awkwardly. He rose early at 4am and the sacrament was administered, then he ate a hearty breakfast at 730am, just half an hour before the execution. It was a drizzly and foggy morning but this didn't deter around 300 morbid people from gathering outside the gaol and waiting for the black flag to be hoisted.

For the first time since 1878 the High Sheriff had allowed journalists in to witness the execution, but limited the number to two, who were allowed in fifteen minutes before it was due to take place. The executioner was Bartholomew Binns, who was carrying out a hanging at Kirkdale for the first time. He stayed at the Sessions House hotel and had arrived at 715am, inexplicably having not sought a pass for his assistant, who was refused entry by officials. When the bell tolled at 750am Dutton was taken to the pinioning room, where Binns carried out the procedure in a clumsy manner, taking considerably longer than Marwood had done.

It was eight minutes before Dutton was ready to be taken on to the scaffold and he stepped up firmly, with Binns placing the rope around his neck and hood over his head whilst the chaplain prayed loudly. Dutton said 'Lord Jesus receive my soul' as the bolt was drawn. Death though was not as instantaneous as it would have been under Marwood. Dutton struggled for a full two minutes writhing around and opening and closing his hands as he was slowly strangled. Prior to the prisoner climbing the scaffold, warders who had witnessed numerous executions commented that the rope was much different in size and shape than they were used to seeing.

Binns was pale when he went down to the body and tried to make out that death had still occurred within three minutes. The doctor disagreed though and said that was only the time the senses became useless and that life was not fully extinct until six minutes after the bolt was drawn. On leaving the gaol for the Sessions House, Binns was asked by reporters why he used a different type of rope and he replied in a thick Yorkshire accent that Marwood's were too thin and liable to snap. He declined to stay for the inquest, claiming his wife was unwell and took a cab with his companion to Lime Street station.

3rd March 1884 – Catherine Flanagan & Margaret Higgins For the Murder of Thomas Higgins at Liverpool

Catherine Flanagan and Margaret Higgins became the first females to be executed at Kirkdale for twelve years and also the first members of the same family to be hanged there. They paid the ultimate price for a crime that earned them a place in the Chamber of Horrors at Madame Tussauds and was described by the *Liverpool Mercury* the day after the execution as 'unrivalled for cold bloodedness, the grovelling animal cunning and the ferocious greed of gain.'

On 4th October 1883 mourners were gathering at 27 Ascot Street in Vauxhall for the funeral of 45 year old hod carrier Thomas Higgins who had died two days earlier, apparently of dysentery with the death having been certified by a doctor. There was a knock at the door which his wife Margaret assumed to be the driver of the hearse, but it was instead a doctor and the coroner's beadle. They had in their possession a warrant preventing the burial from taking place, after Thomas's brother Patrick had reported his suspicions to the police that all was not right.

Patrick had established that his brother's life had been insured to the sum of over £100 with a number of friendly societies in the past few months, with the person who took the policies being not his wife but his sister in law Catherine Flanagan. On seeing the officials, she quickly stopped preparing the shroud and escaped via the back door, briefly returned to her Latimer Street home to collect any incriminating documents before fleeing to the south end of the city.

44 year old Margaret Higgins was arrested on suspicion of being concerned in the death of her husband and police successfully applied for a remand. A post mortem soon established that there was arsenic in the stomach. Although there was no doubt that Thomas had suffered from dysentery, the doctor involved accepted that in his final hours the symptoms he showed were

consistent with arsenic poisoning. Higgins immediately claimed that if her husband had died from poisoning then it had been her sister who had administered it, but an examination of her own clothing found particles of arsenic in an pocket.

On 15th October 54 year old Flanagan was finally apprehended in a boarding house in Mount Vernon Street, where she had booked in using her maiden name of Clifford. Suspicions were aroused by her free spending, her desire to travel to Blackburn and claim that a warrant was out for her arrest for theft, leading to the proprietor calling in the police. The following day both sisters were charged with Thomas's death at the police office. Flanagan said she knew nothing about it and Higgins that he had dysentery and she had been administering the medication that the Burlington Street Dispensary recommended.

Enquiries with local insurance societies established that a number of others had been insured by Flanagan shortly before their deaths. The Home Secretary authorised the exhumation of Margaret Jennings, an 18 year old girl who had lodged with the sisters at a previous address in Skirving Street earlier that year and whose life had been insured by Flanagan. When she was disinterred the body was decomposed, but not as much as would have been expected and particles of arsenic were found in her stomach. Further exhumations took place in January of Thomas Higgins' ten year old daughter Mary and Flanagan's 22 year old son John. Both were found to contain particles of arsenic.

After several remands while the police carefully and meticulously gathered the evidence, the sisters were finally committed to the assizes charged with four murders on 3rd February 1884. Both were charged with the killing of Thomas Higgins and John Flanagan, while Higgins was charged solely with that of her step daughter and Flanagan that of Mary Jennings. The trial opened on 14th February before Mr Justice Butt and was one of the most eagerly awaited ever at St George's Hall, with the *Daily Post* reporting that thousands had to be turned away. On the second day, there was some humour as it was interrupted for a short time when a stout man became stuck between benches whilst trying to leave the courtroom.

As was customary at the time, just one charge was proceeded with, that of the murder of Thomas Higgins. After three days of evidence the prosecution closing arguments were simple, that there was a clear motive and only the two sisters were with Thomas during his final days. In respect of the administration of the poison, Mr Aspinall for the Crown said that one could not possibly have given it without the other knowing. Representing the prisoners, Mr Shee called no witnesses, instead subjecting those called by the prosecution to rigorous cross examination. He maintained that the amount of arsenic found was small and as such there was sufficient doubt which meant a guilty verdict couldn't be returned.

The jury were out for an hour before finding both sisters guilty. In passing sentence, Mr Justice Butt said their crime was so cruel and sordid that he shuddered to think to what depths humanity was sinking. At Kirkdale the sisters were attended to by Father Bonte and appeared penitent, but being unable to read or write made no written confession. They did hint to officials though that they weren't the only people to benefit from killings carried out so that insurance money could be claimed. On the Sunday before the execution they twice had Holy Communion and had a resigned acceptance to their fate. After spending a restless night Higgins offered to make a full confession in the hope of securing a respite but this was refused. Flanagan, to the end, refused to say anything about the crimes.

There was a heavy snowfall on the morning of Monday 3rd March, but that didn't deter a large crowd estimated at 1,000 from gathering near the gates of the gaol. The Mercury described them as 'mainly from the lower classes' and reported that there were many women holding babies there. As opposed to the last execution five pressmen were admitted instead of two, although they were not allowed into the pinioning room and had to observe the walk to the scaffold from the prison yard.

Despite his unease on the previous occasion, Bartholomew Binns was invited back to perform the execution but this time he did make provisions for an assistant, Samuel Heath, to be admitted to the gaol. Both sisters looked old and frail as they were assisted up the 22 steps to the scaffold as the snow continued to come down and there was a biting wind. Father Bonte had an umbrella but struggled to keep it in shape and his prayers could hardly be heard. With a look of resignation on their faces, they barely uttered any responses and didn't look at each other during the whole process.

Binns was far more composed than last time it was less than a minute between the sisters mounting the scaffold and the bolt being drawn. The doctor confirmed that consciousness was lost immediately, although it did take several minutes for the hearts to stop. 24 hours later the two sisters waxwork models were on display at Madame Tussaud's while Binns would be back at Kirkdale a week later where he was once again incompetent.

A week after the execution of Flanagan and Higgins eighteen year Michael McLean was hanged for the brutal kicking to death of a Spanish sailor. It was an execution where due to the hangman's incompetence the killer endured a slow and painful death just like his victim.

On 5th January 1884 at about 10pm two Spaniards called Exequiel Nunez and Jose Jiminez, whose ship the *Serra* was berthed in Canada Dock, were walking along Regent Road when they encountered a group of five youths at the corner with Blackstone Street. One of these was McLean, who was accompanied by Patrick Duggan, Alexander Campbell, Murdoch Ballantyne and William Dempsey.

Ballantyne punched Jiminez without warning but he managed to escape and went to seek help from a policeman, but his friend was now at the mercy of the group. Nunez was then punched and kicked before getting away, but he was pursued to Fulton Street where he was beaten, kicked and stabbed in the neck. Members of a watching crowd went on to say that McLean and either Duggan or Dempsey used knives during the assault. The killers dispersed and a horse drawn ambulance was sent for, but Nunez died on the way to hospital. Due to the notoriety of those involved the five youths were soon apprehended, McLean in possession of a knife and some of the others with blood on their clothing.

At the assizes on 18th February the prosecution opening speeches highlighted the lack of motive for the crime, saying it was just a case of wanton brutality. They contended that if the five youths had banded together for the purpose of committing a felony then all were guilty, irrespective of who had inflicted the fatal wound. A key witness was Esther Ramsden, who saw Duggan hold Nunez down while McLean kicked him. She then told how Duggan asked to wipe his hands on her apron and clarified that Nunez did not appear to have any weapon on him. Another woman Esther Cobley saw Duggan beat him with a belt and McLean kick him in the stomach, but said that Campbell and Dempsey were there but did nothing while Ballantyne was even further away.

The defendants were represented by different counsel who were able to convince the jury that they had not acted as a collective, leading to guilty verdicts being returned on McLean and Duggan only. When they were asked if they had anything to say prior to sentence being passed, both said that it was Dempsey that committed the murder. After being sentenced to death both left the dock with a callous smile on their faces.

Dempsey went on to sign an affidavit stating that he had a knife in his hand on the evening of the murder and had been mistaken for Duggan. This was forwarded to the Home Secretary and as he considered this the execution was postponed, meaning there would be no quadruple execution involving the two males and the poisonous sisters. It was decided to commute Duggan's sentence to penal servitude for life, but there was no reason to intervene in McLean's case. His situation would not have been helped by three other charges he had faced at those assizes, of robbery with violence, assaulting a police constable and wounding. Duggan was told of his reprieve on 6th March, by which time Dempsey had sailed for a new life in San Francisco.

With McLean's last hope of a reprieve gone, he paid close attention to Father Bonte and continued to protest at the unjustness of his sentence. He wrote to his parents saying that both he and Duggan were innocent and warders felt that even Father Bonte had some belief in his claims.

Executioner Bartholomew Binns arrived at the gaol in a state of intoxication on the Saturday before it was scheduled. He immediately fell asleep and when he was roused developed a fighting attitude, leading to the police being called. By the time an inspector and two constables arrived he had calmed down, avoiding the potential embarrassing situation of him being taken into custody. The following day Samuel Heath who had assisted the previous week arrived but Binns chose to ignore his presence and advised that he would be proceeding on his own. Heath would later state that the two had argued on the train back to Dewsbury a week earlier after Binns showed his ropes to numerous passengers.

The morning of Monday 10th March started off with rain and sleet but as 8am drew nearer the sun began to break through the clouds. Outside the gates the crowd was nowhere near as large as that which had gathered a week earlier for the execution of Flanagan and Higgins. At 745am McLean was taken to the pinioning room and stood nonchalantly as Binns got him ready

On reaching the scaffold, McLean broke away from Father Bonte's arm and ran up the steps. He stood in front of the three reporters who had been admitted, who observed that he did not present the usual picture of a condemned man. He was stout and plump in his features, having a powerful build for his age. He then said to the assembled men of the press: 'Gentlemen, I consider it is a disgrace to the police force of Liverpool and to the law of the country that I am going to suffer death and another boy is going to suffer imprisonment for life for a crime of which we are both innocent, as God is my judge.'

Father Bonte recited prayers which McLean repeated but Binns was nervous as he placed the noose around his neck and then put the hood over his head. He then drew the bolt and McLean lost consciousness immediately on dropping, but the heart continued beating for up to thirteen minutes. His face was very discoloured when the body was cut down and at the subsequent inquest the governor Major Legget told the coroner: 'I think that Binns has no idea how to do it scientifically, he puts the rope around the mans neck and hangs him but it is a perfect accident whether it is successful or not.'

Binns denied having been drunk on his arrival, saying he had just had one glass of beer but had been up all night with his sick wife. In reference to how he calculated the drop and size of the rope, he said that it was a matter of opinion as to whether his or others were using he right method. The coroner summed up that the evidence of Major Leggett and the gaol doctor was more credible and the jury went on to recommend the censure of Binns. The issue was raised in the House of Commons, but the Home Secretary told MPs that he had no power to dismiss a hangman, it was instead up to the under sheriffs who did go on to remove him from their lists. Later that year it was revealed in a court case involving him as a witness that he had practiced his hanging techniques on dogs and cats.

19th August 1884 – Peter Cassidy, For the Murder of Mary Cassidy at Bootle

Following the removal of Binns officials at Kirkdale turned to another Yorkshireman, James Berry and the first occasion he was required was for another drink fuelled wife murder. Peter Cassidy said he had killed his wife in retaliation for being struck, but the prosecution were able to prove that there had been a pre-meditation on his part to commit murder anyway.

Cassidy was a 54 year old tinsmith with the Cunard shipping line who lived at 4 Howe Street in Bootle. He had been married to Mary for over twenty years and they had three children, one living in America, one in domestic service in Manchester and the other at an industrial school. The marriage was not always a happy one with both drinking regularly and there were frequent quarrels. Mary often left for brief periods and it was after she had gone to stay with their daughter in Manchester for ten days in June 1884 that the murder was committed.

While Mary was away Cassidy was visited by a man named Mr Swift, whom he was hiring furniture from. Payments had not been kept to and Swift removed the items, promising to return them when the outstanding amount was paid. Mary returned on 25th June but first went to the room of Mr & Mrs McGee, who gave her some tea. When Cassidy heard that she was there he went and angrily confronted her, saying he had even been to Manchester looking for her. He demanded that she return to their room to tidy up but Mary said that she was ill, although she did agree to come up if he helped.

Soon afterwards they went up to their room but when Mr McGee heard two loud thuds he went to investigate and saw Mary lying in a pool of blood with Cassidy next to her. Caught red handed, Cassidy said 'Alright Pat I done it and will stand for it.' Mr McGee went for a policeman and when he arrived and asked Cassidy what happened he produced a bloodied mallet. He was taken into custody and a doctor called who confirmed the death. A search of the room also found a blood covered meat cleaver hidden behind some boards. As he was being transported to the Bridewell he said 'Well I don't know what to say about it I'm sorry it happened.'

After the inquest returned a verdict of wilful murder on 28th June Cassidy appeared at Bootle police court two days later for committal to the assizes. On the same day Mary was interred at St Mary's churchyard, a large crowd singing hymns at the graveside. The only relative present was their daughter who fainted as the coffin was lowered into the grave.

Cassidy appeared before Justice Day at the assizes on 31st July. Mr McGee recalled finding Cassidy standing next to his wife's body while the police officers who were called testified to his responses. Mr Swift who had hired out the furniture told how four days before the killing Cassidy was scathing about his wife's habits and said he would 'do for her.' The doctor who attended said that there was a cut and bruise above Mary's eye which was probably caused by the mallet, but the cause of death was due to a fractured skull, which had been pierced three times by the cleaver.

A statement from Cassidy was put in to the effect that he had been chopping some wood chips when Mary hit him with the mallet, leading to him retaliating with the cleaver and not intending to kill. Several witnesses testified to Cassidy's character and even Mr McGee acknowledged that when the couple weren't in drink he was a kind husband. This though didn't sway the jury who found him guilty of murder but with a recommendation of mercy. Justice Day told him that he would forward the recommendation on but he should not be buoyed by it and then passed the death sentence in the usual form. Cassidy, who had remained motionless throughout the trial, didn't say a word as he was removed from the dock.

Cassidy was attended to at Kirkdale by Father Bonte, to whom he expressed regret at the enormity of his crime. A petition was forwarded to the Home Secretary by many of his friends but he felt there was no reason to interfere with the course of the law. He was reconciled to his fate and his only wish was to have one last visit from his children, which was granted.

Despite the rain on the morning of Tuesday 19th August several hundred morbid onlookers gathered outside the gaol to await the hoisting of the black flag. Pressmen were admitted and they observed Cassidy maintain a remarkable composure, showing no resistance or fear as he was being pinioned. As he mounted the scaffold he quietly repeated the prayers of Father Bonte but had nothing else to say.

At 801am the bolt was pulled and death was instantaneous, with the *Liverpool Mercury* reporting that Berry had performed his functions 'exceedingly well'. He used the same rope width as Marwood had and did not cause any unnecessary alarm as he was going about his duties. At the subsequent inquest the gaol doctor said the execution was the most satisfactory one he had ever witnessed.

1884 was the only year in the history of Kirkdale gaol when executions took place on four separate dates. The last of them was in December when a Manchester man who murdered his wife and a Russian sailor who had killed a Liverpool woman met their fate.

Arthur Shaw was a 31 year old tailor who lived unhappily with his wife Ellen and four year old daughter in Dalton Street in the Collyhurst district of Manchester. In the early hours of 3rd November 1884 a neighbour heard a commotion coming from his property, with his daughter appearing to say 'Dadda don't beat mother.' That evening, Ellen went to Mrs Fletcher's house in the same street to do some knitting. She remained there about an hour and a half until Shaw came to collect her at about 830pm.

Only a minute or so after Ellen had returned home Mrs Fletcher went out on an errand and heard a scream as she passed the Shaw's house. She knocked on the door but got no answer so continued on her errand, returning some time later to find the door open and her own husband and son inside. They had been called in by Shaw who told them that Ellen had fell into a grate. When they went into the house, they saw that Ellen was sat dead in a chair with her eyes and mouth wide open and with bruises by her ears. A policeman was sent for and after the grate was inspected and found not to have been disturbed, Shaw was taken into custody. A doctor who then examined the body found no ash at all and was of the opinion death was as a result of asphyxiation.

At the inquest on 5th November the doctor who carried out the post mortem revealed that the lungs and windpipe were congested and the injuries were not consistent with a fall. In addition to Mr and Mrs Fletcher, former neighbours who remembered the couple from their previous home in Rochdale Road told how Shaw would often be drunk and violent to his wife. It took just a few minutes for a verdict of wilful murder to be found.

Shaw appeared at the Liverpool assizes on 20th November, just seventeen days after the killing. Mr and Mrs Fletcher gave evidence as to them being called into the house by Shaw and another neighbour John Atkin told how he had noticed blood on Ellen's face and a wall. The doctor who attended also described his findings, which were backed up by a medical lecturer who said that there was bruising on the tongue and a tooth had been loosened. In defence, Shaw claimed that his wife had wanted to go back out but he would not let her, so he pushed her and she fell into the grate. In summing up Mr Justice Day said that if death resulted from violence, then the jury must return a murder verdict.

The jury found Shaw guilty but with a recommendation for mercy. When asked if he had anything to say, Shaw replied that he had no intention of hurting his wife, he just wanted his home to be as comfortable as possible and tried to stop her going out. Justice Day did not mince his words, saying: 'No-one could doubt that the jury have not come to a sound conclusion in saying that your wife had been strangled.' He the passed the death sentence in the usual form, saying he would pass the recommendation for mercy on.

The following day at the assizes Ernest Ewerstaedt was sentenced to death for the murder of a local woman who refused to have any more to do with him. The victim was 28 year old Elizabeth Hamblin, a woman described by the Liverpool Mercury as 'of doubtful character' who rented a room in Anson Place, off London Road. She got into a relationship with the 23 year old Russian, who was renting a room in St James Place having not been required for further work after arriving on a sailing from Riga. However Ewerstaedt's poor financial situation led to Hamblin ending the affair, leaving him particularly annoyed as she also appeared to be seeing other men at the same time.

On the 19th September Ewerstaedt went with John Prange who he was lodging with to see Hamblin in Anson Place. Prange went to her room and was told by Hamblin, who was sat talking to two men, that she didn't want to see Ewerstaedt, who reacted angrily and said that he would be buying a gun the next night. Ewerstaedt spent the next afternoon drinking with a fellow Russian sailor named William Gillick and then bought a dagger in Park Lane, but didn't say what he wanted it for. He then headed up to Anson Place on his own after Gillick had gone to his lodgings at the Sailors' Home in Canning Place.

After having a drink with Hamblin and her neighbour in Gildart Street, Ewerstaedt showed them the dagger and said he would do a bloody deed with it that night. Both women then returned to Anson Place, followed by Ewerstaedt a few minutes later. After pacing up and down for some time he knocked but there was no answer so he went to the back entry and climbed over the wall, demanding that Hamblin have more drink with him. He was shown into the parlour but before Hamblin could respond Ewerstaedt plunged the dagger into her breast and she fell down dead, with him leaving the property via the back door.

What Ewerstaedt hadn't realised was that the whole incident had been witnessed by a local ten year old called Henry Titherington who had been intrigued at seeing him walking back and forth outside Hamblin's house. This led to police apprehending Ewerstaedt in the entry, and a search of the house found the body lying face down in the parlour, with the dagger hidden in the water closet.

Thousands of people descended on Anson Place the next day to view the scene of the crime, while further details emerged of

Hamblin's private life. Her landlady said that she had been married four years earlier but her husband had since left for Australia. She had no other family, her parents having died while she was a child, leaving her to be brought up by the Kirkdale Industrial Schools.

At the police court on 22nd September Ewerstaedt didn't ask for an interpreter, explaining that he understood English perfectly well having been living in Liverpool on and off for a year. After hearing the evidence of Henry Titherington, stipendiary magistrate Mr Raffles remanded the prisoner for three days pending an inquest. The following day Henry told the coroner the same thing and another boy, Twelve year old Henry Vecock said he had seen Ewerstaedt demand one and a half pence from Hamblin, threatening to kill her if she did not have it. After medical evidence was produced to say Hamblin was healthy and the wound to the heart was the cause of death, a verdict of wilful murder was returned. Ewerstaedt was then committed to the assizes for trial, with him claiming at the committal hearing that he was drunk on the night of the murder and was fighting with two men who had daggers, but he was not responsible for the killing.

On 24th September Hamblin's funeral was due to took place but as the procession was on its way to the cemetery it was called back to Anson Place. Her body was then removed from the workhouse coffin and placed in another one which had been paid for by other women in the neighbourhood. She was then interred at the graveyard of the church of St Martins in the Fields three days later.

Ewerstaedt was tried on 21st November, with the Russian consul being in attendance to assist wherever necessary. The prosecutor described him as a 'Russian Finn while the *Liverpool Echo* said he was of 'inoffensive appearance' and listened to the proceedings with 'not the slightest interest.' Both his fellow sailors gave evidence that helped condemn him, in that Gillick said he was present when the dagger was bought and Prange said Ewerstaedt had threatened to buy a revolver. A shopkeeper confirmed he had sold the dagger for two shillings and although he couldn't identify Ewerstaedt he knew the buyer was foreign. Neighbours in Anson Place told how they had seen Ewerstaedt produce it in the pub and another female said that she saw a man shout 'Me kill my Lizzie' on the corner of Anson Place and London Road. Ten year old Henry Titherington repeated his evidence from the first court hearing.

The Defence counsel Mr Segar had an uphill task in persuading the jury to acquit his client. He described how Ewerstaedt had woken on the Sunday morning believing the whole thing was like a dream in which he had been fighting with two men. Segar stated that Titherington's evidence was unreliable due his age and anything else was purely circumstantial, laying the blame for the murder on two men who had not been caught. But with not a single witness able to put two unknown men in Anson Place on the night of the murder, Mr Justice Day's summing up was not favourable to Ewerstaedt. After returning a verdict of guilty, he was sentenced to death and taken to Kirkdale gaol.

Ewerstaedt spent a lonely three weeks awaiting execution, not receiving a single visitor apart from the Reverend Gerald Krusmann from the Lutheran Church in Renshaw Street. He continued to maintain his innocence, sticking to his claim about the two other males. The *Manchester Courier* observed though that he was so 'madly intoxicated' at the time that he could have had no recollection anyway. In contrast, Shaw accepted he had killed his wife, but continued to state he had not intended to. He was attended to by gaol chaplain Octavius Pigott, to whom he admitted that he had led an immoral life. He had hopes of a reprieve and petitions were signed in Manchester and forwarded to the Home Secretary, but he saw no reason to interfere with the law.

With this being the fourth execution of the year, there was not as much interest as before and less than a hundred idlers waited around outside the gaol walls for the black flag to be hoisted. Inside the prisoners seemed to witness the enormity of their situation as they were led to the pinioning room. Shaw had his arms clasped together and Ewerstaedt's head was bowed. Both walked steadily onto the scaffold, praying loudly. They continued to do so as James Berry and his assistant Mr Speight put the white caps over their heads and were still seeking forgiveness as the bolt was drawn.

Against usual convention the newly appointed county coroner Mr Brighouse opted to hold the inquest at 11am rather than as soon as the bodies were cut down. It was revealed that Ewerstaedt's death was instant but Shaw had struggled for about a minute due to him not dropping properly, there having been a fault with the door flap. Berry said he had asked for a repair but the gaol engineer testified that he had not been given the instruction. The governor Major Leggett though said that the execution was within the law which said 'hanged by the neck until dead'. Although dislocation of the neck was desirable as it hastened death, it was not a prerequisite and the usual verdict that the law had been carried out in a proper manner was returned.

A year to the day after Ernest Ewerstaedt was only the third
person from outside the British Isles to be executed at Kirkdale,
George Thomas became the fourth. The sailor from Guyana was
hanged for the killing of a woman at Toxteth in a murder that was
motivated by jealousy.

32 year old Thomas arrived in Liverpool on 3rd September 1885
on board the *Mary L. Barel* which had sailed from Bombay. He
had been away nearly a year but after being paid his wages for
the voyage he went to stay with widow Margaret Askin who lived
in Brassey Street, Toxteth, which was his usual custom when he
was in Liverpool. Askin, who was two years younger than
Thomas was described by the *Liverpool Mercury* as being 'of the
most disreputable class.'

On 8th September another seaman named Louis Powell arrived
at the house and a fight took place, in which Thomas produced a
knife. The following afternoon he had an argument, fuelled by
jealousy, with Margaret (known as Maggie) who had asked him
for money to buy food for Powell. During this row Thomas had a
cup thrown at him while Powell kicked him as he fell down in the
street. Margaret had pawned some of Thomas's clothes and a
watch that he had left when he had last stayed there and when
he got the ticket back for the watch he exchanged it for a
revolver.

That evening Thomas asked Margaret, her friend Mrs Tipping
and Powell to accompany him to a pub at the corner of
Harrington Street and Beaufort Street for a drink. Powell refused
but the two ladies went with him, Thomas asking Mrs Tipping to
return and try and persuade him to come out. When Mrs Tipping
was away doing this, Thomas shot at Margaret in full view of
other customers. She was shouting 'Oh I am shot' as Mrs
Tipping returned and Thomas then shot Margaret in the forehead

and mouth, leading to her collapsing and dying instantly. He then turned then gun on himself and lay down and put his arm around Margaret.

The pub landlord ran out and blew a whistle to attract the attention of police and when they arrived Maggie was already dead but Thomas was fully conscious with blood pouring from a wound behind his ear. He was taken to the Southern Hospital where he admitted shooting Margaret dead and then turning the gun on himself. An operation was performed to remove the bullet and the next day he was discharged and taken to the Bridewell. In a reflection of how non whites were seen then, press reports into the case constantly reported that Thomas was 'coloured', with the *Leeds Times* even saying he was a 'darky.'

The inquest took place on 11th September and after a verdict of wilful murder was returned Thomas was committed for trial at the assizes, where he appeared before Mr Justice Wills on 16th November. The only defence that his counsel could come up with was temporary insanity but this was not accepted and the jury returned a guilty verdict after about ten minutes. When asked if he had anything to say Thomas replied: 'All I can say is that I am sorry I did not shoot the whole family.' As Justice Wills said there was no doubt he had bought the revolver with the intention of killing Margaret, Thomas replied: 'Correct My Lord.' After the death sentence was passed he said 'Praise God for that I shall have no more suffering on Earth.'

Thomas was attended to by the goal chaplain Octavius Pigott and showed great remorse for his crime, saying that he simply could not hold his passion. He was a member of the Church of England and showed great knowledge of the Bible in his conversations. The last sacrament was taken on Sunday 6th December and he remained very quiet the next day, his last full one on Earth. After going to bed after midnight he slept soundly until 6am and rose, refusing breakfast and opting only for a cup of tea.

Members of the press were admitted at the same time as Thomas was being led to the pinioning room. He walked collectedly to where the executioner James Berry was waiting for him. Due to the mishap that had happened a year before Berry had tested the trapdoor on his arrival and was satisfied that there would be no problems. Thomas continued praying loudly as he went onto the scaffold and he said to those present: 'Take warning from me all you young men. Beware of the sins of adultery and murder. I have committed a grievous sin in the sight of God.' He then clasped his hands and continued praying as he dropped, when death was instantaneous. Outside a crowd of around 100 began to disperse once the black flag was hoisted.

It would be six years before the next and ultimately last hanging at Kirkdale gaol took place, when marine fireman John Conway was executed for the motiveless murder of a boy he found playing in the street.

As a county gaol Kirkdale was becoming redundant following the Prison Act of 1877, which centralised the control of prisons. Walton, which had opened in the 1850s and built on the panopticon principle which was believed to make it easier to observe inmates, was now emerging as the main prison for the Liverpool area.

In 1887 the gallows were transferred from Kirkdale to Walton for the hanging of Elizabeth Berry who had poisoned her daughter to claim an insurance policy. They looked set to remain there until they were needed back at Kirkdale in 1891, by which time there were only around fifty prisoners left at the gaol. The condemned man that they were taken back for John Conway was convicted on purely circumstantial evidence but it was so overwhelming that there was no doubt as to his guilt.

The last time ten year old Nicholas Martin was seen by any of his family was at 845pm on the evening of Saturday 16th May 1891, when he was playing ball outside his house in Bridgewater Street. His mother went to some shops and when she returned half an hour later he was nowhere to be seen. However, as he had a habit of going to an uncle's house in Great Howard Street his disappearance wasn't reported to the police until the Monday.

The following morning two gatemen at the Sandon Dock pulled a black bag out of the water and found that it contained the badly mutilated body of Nicholas, his feet having been cut off. Word soon got around the city of the find and the boy's father, also called Nicholas, identified the body at a mortuary that evening.

Enquiries focused on the black canvass bag that the body had been placed in and it was soon found that it had been sold from a shop in Park Lane on the Monday afternoon. The woman there gave a description of the man and further enquiries locally led to the arrest of sixty year old John Conway at a lodging house in Bridgewater Street on the Wednesday evening. He was taken to the central police office in Dale Street where the woman who sold him the bag picked him out of an identity parade. She also told police he had bought a blanket from her, in which Nicholas's body had been wrapped.

Conway was the local representative of the Sailors' Union and the following day investigations centred on his office at 19 Stanhope Street. Blood was found on floorboards and the ceiling, leading police to conclude that even if the murder had not taken place there, the butchery of the body had. Four boys then came forward to say they had seen Conway take a cab from Stanhope Street at about 930pm on the Monday night, whilst carrying a black canvass bag. One of the boys offered to carry it in the hope of earning a penny but was brushed aside and the cab driver was declined when he offered assistance on arrival at the George's Dock landing stage, where it was supposed the bag was dumped in the River Mersey.

At the inquest on Friday 22nd May Nicholas's mother was so distressed at the description of his body that she had to go and sit in the coroner's room. The jury visited the offices in Stanhope Street then returned a verdict of wilful murder. Conway appeared at the police court to be committed to the assizes, screaming 'My God my God I am not guilty.' He admitted buying the bag and blankets but said he had no knowledge of how Nicholas's body had come to be in them. On the Sunday, Nicholas's funeral was held at the Church of St Vincent de Paul followed by a procession to Ford Cemetery where he was buried.

Conway had been known locally for about fifteen years and officials of the union were aghast that he could have committed such a heinous crime and offered to pay for his defence. He had been at sea for thirty years and was a veteran of the Crimean War, having spoken fondly of his role in the Battle of Inkerman.

Conway's trial took place on the 31st July and 1st August. Fellow boarding house lodgers identified the razor which was believed to be the murder weapon as having belonged to him. The boys who had seen him carrying the bag to a cab, the driver and woman from the shop all gave evidence that went against him. Conway's defence was that the murder had been committed by an unknown foreign sailor who had made enquiries about joining the union. His defence counsel pointed out that he had no motive, knew Nicholas's parents and had been drinking and acting normally with friends on the Sunday. It was barely credible they said, that he could lead such a flawless life for sixty years then turn into a monster.

In summing up the judge said the evidence pointed to the killing having taken place in Stanhope Street and asked the jury to consider one crucial point. If Conway hadn't committed the murder, he must instead have gone to the office on the Monday morning and found the body so if that was the case why hadn't he called the police. It took the jury half an hour to reach a verdict of guilty and Conway said nothing as sentence of death was passed in the normal form. A large crowd gathered at the northern entrance of St George's Hall as he was then taken to Kirkdale gaol in a cab.

On the day before the execution Conway finally confessed to the crime, writing out a statement which Father Bonte released to the press. He wrote: 'I was impelled to the crime whilst under the influence of drink by a fit of murderous mania and a morbid curiosity to observe the process of dying. A moment after the commission of the crime I experienced the deepest horror of it and would have done anything in the world to undo it.'

Conway sighed many times as he slowly climbed the scaffold and then shook hands with the executioner James Berry, saying 'God bless you.' As the white cap was being placed over his head Conway said 'Hold on I want to say something' and Father Bonte urged Berry to allow him to do so. Taking a deep breath the condemned man said: 'Beware of drink, I want to speak of the prison officials they were very kind to me. I wish all my prosecutors to be forgiven by me and God.' As he then repeatedly said 'Of Lord have mercy on my soul' Berry pulled the bolt and Conway dropped to his death.

Death had been instant but had not occurred in a satisfactory manner. There was a great deal of blood under the body which had almost been decapitated. Berry had miscalculated the drop for the second time in two days, having the previous day badly cut the neck of a man he was hanging at Bermondsey. He left Kirkdale straight away rather than attend the inquest and on his return to Bradford he refused to speak to any visitors to his home. The following day the *Liverpool Mercury* published a letter from a shocked Charles Poll of Union Court, who felt that 'It is time something was done to abolish such a barbarous system of capital punishment and adopt some more humane and decent way of carrying out the death penalty.'

The hanging of Conway would turn out to be the last execution at Kirkdale. Six months later on 16th February 1892 the last two prisoners there, who had tended to the gardens and dug Berry's grave, were transferred to Walton. There would be no more executions for Berry either, who resigned his post in March 1892 having been overlooked by the sheriffs for any required executions since the Conway mishap. James Billington would initially take over at Walton where over sixty murderers were hanged prior to the death penalty's abolition in 1964.

Further Reading

Tod Sloan: The Treadmill & The Rope – The History of a Liverpool Prison (The Gallery Press 1988)

John Smith: The Register of Death – A History of Execution at Walton Prison (Countyvise 2007)

Steve Fielding: Hanged at Liverpool (The History Press 2008)

John E Archer: The Monster Evil – Policing and Violence in Victorian Liverpool (Liverpool University Press 2011)

Michael McIlwee: The Liverpool Underworld – Crime in the City 1750-1900 (Liverpool University Press 2011)

Printed in Great Britain
by Amazon

38639244R00056